Ten Lectures on Figurative Meaning-Making: The Role of Body and Context

Distinguished Lectures in Cognitive Linguistics

Edited by
Fuyin (Thomas) Li (*Beihang University, Beijing*)

Guest Editor
Yan Ding (*Beijing Jiaotong University*)

Editorial Assistants
Jing Du, Na Liu and Cuiying Zhang (*doctoral students at Beihang University*)

Editorial Board
Jürgen Bohnemeyer (*State University of New York at Buffalo*) – Alan Cienki (*Vrije Universiteit (VU), Amsterdam, Netherlands and Moscow State Linguistic University, Russia*) – William Croft (*University of New Mexico at Albuquerque, USA*) – Ewa Dąbrowska (*Northumbria University, UK*) – Gilles Fauconnier (*University of California at San Diego, USA*) – Dirk Geeraerts (*University of Leuven, Belgium*) – Nikolas Gisborne (*The University of Edinburgh, UK*) – Cliff Goddard (*Griffith University, Australia*) – Stefan Gries (*University of California, Santa Barbara, USA*) – Laura A. Janda (*University of Tromsø, Norway*) – Zoltán Kövecses (*Eötvös Loránd University, Hungary*) – George Lakoff (*University of California at Berkeley, USA*) – Ronald W. Langacker (*University of California at San Diego, USA*) – Chris Sinha (*Hunan University, China*) – Leonard Talmy (*State University of New York at Buffalo, USA*) – John R. Taylor (*University of Otago, New Zealand*) – Mark Turner (*Case Western Reserve University, USA*) – Sherman Wilcox (*University of New Mexico, USA*) – Phillip Wolff (*Emory University, USA*) Jeffrey M. Zacks (*Washington University, USA*)

Distinguished Lectures in Cognitive Linguistics publishes the keynote lectures series given by prominent international scholars at the China International Forum on Cognitive Linguistics since 2004. Each volume contains the transcripts of 10 lectures under one theme given by an acknowledged expert on a subject and readers have access to the audio recordings of the lectures through links in the e-book and QR codes in the printed volume. This series provides a unique course on the broad subject of Cognitive Linguistics. Speakers include George Lakoff, Ronald Langacker, Leonard Talmy, Laura Janda, Dirk Geeraerts, Ewa Dąbrowska and many others.

The titles published in this series are listed at *brill.com/dlcl*

Ten Lectures on Figurative Meaning-Making: The Role of Body and Context

By

Zoltán Kövecses

BRILL

LEIDEN | BOSTON

The Library of Congress Cataloging-in-Publication Data is available online at http://catalog.loc.gov

Typeface for the Latin, Greek, and Cyrillic scripts: "Brill". See and download: brill.com/brill-typeface.

ISSN 2468-4872
ISBN 978-90-04-36489-9 (hardback)
ISBN 978-90-04-36490-5 (e-book)

Copyright 2020 by Zoltán Kövecses. Reproduced with kind permission from the author by Koninklijke Brill NV, Leiden, The Netherlands.
Koninklijke Brill NV incorporates the imprints Brill, Brill Hes & De Graaf, Brill Nijhoff, Brill Rodopi, Brill Sense, Hotei Publishing, mentis Verlag, Verlag Ferdinand Schöningh and Wilhelm Fink Verlag.
All rights reserved. No part of this publication may be reproduced, translated, stored in a retrieval system, or transmitted in any form or by any means, electronic, mechanical, photocopying, recording or otherwise, without prior written permission from the publisher.
Authorization to photocopy items for internal or personal use is granted by Koninklijke Brill NV provided that the appropriate fees are paid directly to The Copyright Clearance Center, 222 Rosewood Drive, Suite 910, Danvers, MA 01923, USA. Fees are subject to change.

This book is printed on acid-free paper and produced in a sustainable manner.

*With many thanks to Olga Boryslavska
for all her help*

Contents

Note on Supplementary Material IX
Preface X
About the Author XII

1 Recent Challenges to Conceptual Metaphor Theory 1

2 Metaphorical Meaning Making: Discourse, Language, and Culture 14

3 Metaphor, Culture, and Embodiment 29

4 Emotions I: A Cognitive Linguistic Theory 42

5 Emotions II: Life and Happiness 54

6 Metonymy: A New Look 66

7 A New View of Metaphorical Creativity I 76

8 A New View of Metaphorical Creativity II 88

9 Metaphor and Metonymy in Language Teaching 102

10 Theories of Metaphor: A Synthesis 115

About the Series Editor 125
Websites for Cognitive Linguistics and CIFCL Speakers 126

Note on Supplementary Material

All original audio-recordings and other supplementary material, such as handouts and PowerPoint presentations for the lecture series, have been made available online and are referenced via unique DOI numbers on the website www.figshare.com. They may be accessed via a QR code for the print version of this book. In the e-book both the QR code and dynamic links will be available which can be accessed by a mouse-click.

The material can be accessed on figshare.com through a PC internet browser or via mobile devices such as a smartphone or tablet. To listen to the audio recording on hand-held devices, the QR code that appears at the beginning of each chapter should be scanned with a smart phone or tablet. A QR reader/scanner and audio player should be installed on these devices. Alternatively, for the e-book version, one can simply click on the QR code provided to be redirected to the appropriate website.

This book has been made with the intent that the book and the audio are both available and usable as separate entities. Both are complemented by the availability of the actual files of the presentations and material provided as hand-outs at the time these lectures were given. All rights and permission remain with the authors of the respective works, the audio-recording and supplementary material are made available in Open Access via a CC-BY-NC license and are reproduced with kind permission from the authors. The recordings are courtesy of the China International Forum on Cognitive Linguistics (http://cifcl.buaa.edu.cn/), funded by the Beihang University Grant for International Outstanding Scholars.

 The complete collection of lectures by Zoltán Kövecses can be accessed by scanning this QR code.

© ZOLTÁN KÖVECSES. REPRODUCED WITH KIND PERMISSION FROM THE AUTHOR BY KONINKLIJKE BRILL NV, LEIDEN, 2020 | DOI:10.1163/9789004364905_001

Preface

The present text, entitled *Ten Lectures on Figurative Meaning-Making: The Role of Body and Context* by Zoltán Kövecses, is a transcribed version of the lectures given by Professor Zoltán Kövecses in November 2010 as one of the three forum speakers for *The 8th China International Forum on Cognitive Linguistics*.

The text is published, accompanied by its videodisc counterpart and Chinese guide, as one of the *Eminent Linguists Lecture Series*.

The China International Forum on Cognitive Linguistics provides a forum for eminent international scholars to talk to Chinese audiences. It is a continuing program organized by nine prestigious universities in Beijing. The main organizing institution is Beihang University (BUAA); co-sponsors for CIFCL 8 include Tsinghua University, Peking University, Beijing Foreign Studies University, and Beijing Forestry University. Professor Kövecses's lecture series was mainly supported by *the Beihang Grant for International Outstanding Scientists* for 2010 (Project number: Z1057, Project organizer: Thomas Fuyin Li).

The transcription of the video, proofreading the text, writing the Chinese guide, and publication of the work in its present book form, have involved many people's strenuous inputs. The initial drafts were done by the following postgraduate students from Beihang Univcersity: Chao Chen, Miaomiao Dou, Rong Han, Fan Tian, Dongfang Wang, Yue Wu, Na Yang, Zuan Zhang, Jingyuan Zhao, Xueqing Zhou. Then we editors did the word-by-word and line-by-line revision. To improve the readability of the text, we deleted some of the false starts, repetitions, fillers like *now, so, you know, OK, and so on, again, of course, if you like, sort of*, etc. Occasionally, the written version needs an additional word to be clear, a word that was not actually spoken in the lecture. We've added such words within single brackets [...]. To make the written version readable, even without watching the film, we've added a few "stage instructions", in italics also within single brackets: [...]. The stage instruction describes what the speaker was doing, such as pointing at a slide, showing an object, etc. The speaker, professor Kövecses did the final word-by-word revision. The published version is the final version approved by the speaker.

The publication of this book is sponsored by the Humanities and Social Sciences Research Program Funds of the Chinese Ministry of Education (Number: 09YJA740010).

Thomas Fuyin Li
Beihang University (BUAA)
thomasli@buaa.edu.cn

Yan Ding
Beijing Jiaotong University (BJTU)
yanding@bjtu.edu.cn

About the Author

Zoltán Kövecses is Professor Emeritus in the Department of American Studies, Eötvös Loránd University, Budapest, Hungary. He holds the academic degrees of PhD and DSc.

His main research interests include the conceptualization of emotions, the study of metaphor and idiomaticity, the relationship between language, mind and culture, the role of context in metaphor production, the various levels of schematicity in conceptual metaphor, and American slang and American English.

He has taught and lectured widely at several American, Asian, and European universities, including the University of Nevada at Las Vegas, Rutgers University, University of Massachusetts at Amherst, Hamburg University, Odense University, the University of California at Berkeley, Charles University, Prague, University of Brno, Heidelberg University, Paris Diderot, Sichuan University, Chengdu, Southwest University, Chongqing, Chulalonghorn University, Bangkok, and Srinakharinwirot University, Bangkok.

He has supervised more than a dozen completed PhD dissertations and served on many PhD dissertation committees both in Hungary and abroad.

He is editor of Cognitive Linguistic Studies (with Xu Wen), associate editor of Cognitive Linguistics and Metaphor and Symbol. He also serves on the advisory board of several scholarly journals including Review of Cognitive Linguistics, Cognitive Semantics, and Jezikoslovlje.

His major publications include: *Metaphor and Emotion* (2000, Cambridge UP), *American English: An Introduction* (2000, Broadview Press), *Metaphor: A Practical Introduction* (2002/2010, Oxford UP), *Metaphor in Culture* (2005, Cambridge UP), *Language, Mind, and Culture* (2006, Oxford UP), and *Where Metaphors Come From* (2015, Oxford UP).

In addition to his work in cognitive linguistics, he has been the editor of several general Hungarian-English and English-Hungarian dictionaries. He is also the editor of several specialized dictionaries of English and Hungarian slang, idiomatic language, and British-American differences.

Most recently, he is working on a new book on conceptual metaphor theory.

Prof. Kövecses lives in Budapest, Hungary. His hobby is working in his lakeside orchard and making plum jam – without added sugar and preservatives.

LECTURE 1

Recent Challenges to Conceptual Metaphor Theory

Good morning! I want to thank the organizers, especially Thomas Li, for inviting me here. It is a great opportunity for me to visit your wonderful city—this place is an amazing combination of old and the new things. I'm really enjoying my stay. I hope I can also give you something that can benefit your own purposes.

As you may know, my particular interest is in metaphor theory, but not only theoretical issues in metaphor, but the combination of what metaphor theory can contribute to our understanding of culture, and more generally, to understand how we make sense of the world by means of figurative devices like metaphor and metonymy. In this first introductory lecture, I want to concentrate on the theory of conceptual metaphor—as it was first proposed by Lakoff and Johnson in 1980—and look at some of the criticisms of this theory. In the past 30 years, there has been an accumulating body of criticisms of the Lakoff and Johnson view, which I consider and take to be the "standard conceptual theory" view. What I will do now is to look at some of the criticisms that have been leveled against their theory and try to respond to those criticisms, and on that basis, offer an alternative view to the standard conceptual metaphor theory first proposed by Lakoff and Johnson.

I have some very basic goals this morning and I also have some very ambitious ones. The basic one is that I will go through some of the main ideas of conceptual metaphor theory. I will look at some of the criticisms and then I will try to interpret these criticisms and respond to them. In the process, I will try to come up with an alternative view to what we can take to be the standard theory. I will make use of many of the same ideas that I will introduce today in later lectures, for understanding the larger cultural issues that I will be dealing with.

 All original audio-recordings and other supplementary material, such as any hand-outs and powerpoint presentations for the lecture series, have been made available online and are referenced via unique DOI numbers on the website www.figshare.com. They may be accessed via a QR code for the print version of this book. In the e-book, both the QR code and dynamic links are available, and can be accessed by a mouse-click.

© ZOLTÁN KÖVECSES. REPRODUCED WITH KIND PERMISSION FROM THE AUTHOR BY KONINKLIJKE BRILL NV, LEIDEN, 2020 | DOI:10.1163/9789004364905_002

So there are five major issues that I want to look at, five major criticisms of conceptual metaphor theory and you can follow, you can see the criticisms. The five criticisms include the issue of methodology, the issue of the direction of analysis, the issue of schematicity, the issue of embodiment, and the issue of the relationship with culture. These are the five issues I will take up one by one. I will look at the criticism itself, try to respond to these challenges and offer some kind of alternative to the standard Lakoff and Johnson view. In general, I would say that I very much work in the spirit of the standard Lakoff and Johnson view. However, in the past twenty years, I have made all kinds of suggestions that I think should be made a part of an even stronger theory of conceptual metaphor than what is available today.

Let's turn to the first issue—the issue of methodology. There are basically two kinds of criticisms here. One says that people who work along the lines of standard conceptual metaphor theory work with intuitive examples. That is, if you are a native speaker of English, if you are a native speaker of Chinese, if you are a native speaker of Hungarian, you know some metaphorical linguistic expressions or you find them in a dictionary. On the basis of those metaphorical expressions, you will say you generalize on that basis, and you will say that you have a particular conceptual metaphor. So if for example, in Hungarian, or Chinese or English, there are expressions where, for example, the word "boil" means to be very angry, or "to explode" means to lose control of your anger and so on and so forth, you will generalize and say, well, there is a conceptual metaphor; something like ANGER IS A HOT FLUID IN A CONTAINER. The problem with this, the critics say rightly that these are very intuitive ways of saying first of all "what is a metaphor?". That is, the person who does metaphor analysis assumes in advance what the metaphor is. There is no systematic procedure to identify what metaphors are.

The second kind of objection along the methodology line is to say that well, there is a problem with the way Lakoff and Johnson and their ardent followers are looking at de-contextualized examples of metaphors. We are not looking at real discourse where the metaphors actually occur. Just because I'm not a native speaker, I assume them to be proper contexts. But I'm a dictionary person, I love dictionaries, and I find all kinds of metaphorical expressions and I take them out and I make generalization and come up with the conceptual metaphor. They say this is not an acceptable practice because you have to look at real discourse.

Ok, so this is the way I would respond to these criticisms. I will say that metaphors, first of all, exist on three different levels: The level of the supra-individual; the level of the individual level, and the sub-individual level. The supra-individual level is the one where you have de-contextualized metaphorical expressions like in a dictionary. The dictionary belongs to everyone. You don't even have to be a native speaker. You can look up words in a dictionary, you can find them, you can make generalizations, and come up with conceptual metaphors—this is what I mean by the supra-individual level. They are shared metaphors in a particular language community or culture community. The individual level, however, is the one where real people, actual people, actually use particular metaphorical expressions in particular discourses.

The sub-individual level simply means the level where we find the motivation for the existence of conceptual metaphors and also of linguistic examples of those conceptual metaphors. This is the level where, as we say in Cognitive Linguistics, we find motivation, either bodily or cultural motivation for particular conceptual metaphors.

Now in my view, the response that we can give to the criticism that I mentioned before is that somehow they are working on a different level of analysis where standard conceptual metaphor theory people do. So I feel that I am working at the supra-individual level, the dictionaries, to simplify, the dictionary level. These are de-contextualized metaphorical expressions on the basis of which I come up with the conceptual metaphors. However, the critics work at the individual level. At the individual level, they say that, there are particular discourses that Lakoff and others disregard and it is at the individual level where we should make decisions about what counts as a metaphorical expression. I am working at the supra-individual level, which is the level of de-contextualized metaphorical expressions as opposed to the individual level where you have the contextualized real examples of metaphor use in discourses. Of course, I completely agree with the criticism if we decide to work at the individual level. However, I feel that it is just as important to work at the supra-individual level. So in a way, to criticize one approach that looks at metaphor at a particular level from the perspective of another approach that looks at metaphor at a different level. My point is that there is a mixing of different levels of the existence of metaphor that the critics don't usually keep in mind. Obviously I have no problem at all with looking at metaphor at the individual level, looking at real discourse, coming up with metaphor identification protocols, and so on. This is by the way the job of a group of metaphor theoreticians called the "Pragglejaz Group." The Pragglejaz Group works exactly on this, on this individual level where the major question is what is a metaphor and how can we decide what is a metaphorical linguistic expression.

As a matter of fact, I agree with this kind of attitude to metaphor analysis so much that I am a part of that group as well. But in my view, you have to do both. You have to do metaphor analysis not just on the individual level, but also on the supra-individual level, and also of course at the sub-individual level. You cannot criticize people doing metaphor analysis on one level from the perspective of another level of analysis. We have to somehow integrate the three—that's the major challenge and should be the major goal.

When referring to the direction of analysis, I simply mean whether you do metaphor analysis as a top-down or bottom-up process. If you conduct metaphor analysis with a top-down process, then on the basis of a few intuitive examples, you can come up with a particular conceptual metaphor and then you consider the usual things, work out the mappings, work out the entailments and so on so forth, in a kind of de-contextualized fashion. If you do metaphor analysis bottom-up, then you start with the meticulous examination of particular linguistic expressions in particular discourses. Notice how close this kind of bottom-up and top-down approach issue is to the previous issue that I was talking about.

Now there are two objections that people who work bottom-up in conceptual metaphor theory raise in connection with those who do metaphor analysis top-down. The first assumes a particular conceptual metaphor then sees what kinds of linguistic expressions they can find for that conceptual metaphor. The particular example of this kind of criticism can be found in Dobrovolskij and Piirainen. They wrote a book in 2005 that discusses these issues in great detail and they raise two objections concerning the top-down approach. The first objection that they make is that in the top-down approach, people don't pay enough attention to the huge amount of irregularity in the behavior of particular metaphorical expressions; if you work bottom-up, as I said previously, you look at particular metaphorical expressions and then you look at the details of the semantics of what this metaphor means in a particular context, what are the subtle shades of meanings that are conveyed by a particular metaphorical expression. The argument is that if you have a top-down approach to metaphor analysis, you miss most of those because you will find large overarching regularities instead of irregularities. This is a principle I call "the dominance of irregularity" here. Bottom-up people emphasize the dominance of irregularity and they say that people who work top-down simply disregard all those irregularities and they are missing most of what is important about the meaning—the semantics of particular metaphorical expressions.

To be honest, maybe you'll be surprised to hear this, I have sympathy for this kind of criticism and maybe I am one of the few top-down people in metaphor analysis who would say that yes, there is room for great improvement in this. I do not want to suggest that each and every metaphorical expression we can arrive at can be generalized as a conceptual metaphor—as a global conceptual metaphor. So if you take, for example, the expression "split hairs", I find it is very difficult to come up with any global conceptual metaphor for this. Maybe if I look for days or weeks or months, I could come up with something, but it seems to be much easier to find an overarching global conceptual metaphor for expressions like "boil with anger" and "to lay the foundations of a theory" and the examples of LIFE IS A JOURNEY and so on and so forth. So there are indeed a lot of cases where we can find global conceptual metaphors behind, or underlying or explaining particular metaphorical expressions. But on the other hand, there seems to be many and I couldn't tell you the exact figures nor could I give you any statistics. There are many metaphorical linguistic expressions like "split hairs" where it would be quite difficult to come up with a particular conceptual metaphor. So in a way, I agree with the bottom-up people that it is not the case that all the conceptual, or rather all the metaphorical linguistic expressions that we find can be neatly captured by and explained by overarching, higher level cognitive structures like LIFE IS A JOURNEY, ANGER IS A HOT FLUID, THEORIES ARE BUILDING, and so on and so forth. "Split hairs", is a good example for that.

However, I disagree with the criticism that conceptual metaphor theory in the standard view is simply incapable of explaining what the bottom-up people take to be irregularities. So I think the bottom-up people, when they come up with the notion of the dominance of irregularities in metaphorical expressions, it's an exaggerated claim. I do not think that, although again I don't have statistical evidence, and this could be a further topic for anyone to explore, I don't know what the percentage of those metaphors is that are easily given systematic explanation in terms of conceptual metaphors and those that cannot be explained that way.

So, let's take two expressions like "add fuel to the fire" and "flare up". For "add fuel to the fire", an example could be: "His stupid comment just *added fuel to the fire*"; and for "flare up", an example could be "the argument *flared up* between them." Now if we look at these two metaphorical expressions, the question is, do they behave in an irregular way? Bottom-up people would probably say that they do. The specific meaning of the two expressions cannot be captured by simply proposing a conceptual metaphor to the effect that ANGER IS FIRE. If you stop at the level of proposing a global metaphor like ANGER IS FIRE, then of course you cannot really explain what is going on here. The two authors that I quote here basically say that there is more irregularity than regularity in metaphor.

These two people assume that all that conceptual metaphor analysis takes is that you come up with a source domain and a target domain. Once you establish that, you have done your job. Of course, if this is your only level of analysis in conceptual metaphor theory, then it is impossible to explain what these particular metaphorical expressions mean. But of course, conceptual metaphor theory doesn't stop there. One of the main things that we need to do in the case of all conceptual metaphors like ANGER IS FIRE is to come up with a systematic set of mappings and check to see how systematic that particular correspondence is between anger and fire. As a matter of fact, the ANGER IS FIRE metaphor, in my view, is a more specific version of a higher-level metaphor that I would call INTENSITY IS HEAT. INTENSITY IS HEAT has us go one generalization higher and that higher generalization gives us, I think, a huge amount of explanatory power when we try to specify what the particular meanings of particular metaphorical expressions are.

So the INTENSITY IS HEAT metaphor and the mappings for this are laid out in the handout: The degree of heat corresponds to the degree of intensity, the cause of heat to the cause of intensity, increasing the degree of heat to the increasing degree of intensity, decrease to decrease, and heat dropping to zero corresponds to intensity ceasing. Now given these particular mappings, we can get pretty close to the meanings of such expressions as "add fuel to the fire", and "flare up". We can say for example that the "add fuel to the fire" metaphor is based on the mapping THE CAUSE OF HEAT IS THE CAUSE OF INTENSITY. If you add more fuel to something burning, it will cause more intensity. And "flare up", increasing the degree of heat, increasing the degree of intensity. So when your fire flares up, it indicates more intensity conceptually. So I am not saying we can explain each and every detail of the meaning of these two expressions by means of first setting up a conceptual metaphor ANGER IS FIRE, then setting up the more general INTENSITY IS HEAT, then specifying the mappings between intensity and heat. But we can get pretty close to it. So this is what I mean when I say that I see a lot more regularity in the meaning of metaphorical expressions than what the proponents of the "dominance of irregularities" principle suggests.

The second objection that is raised in connection with the top-down approach is that the people who object to the top-down approach would say that instead of first looking at and finding all the metaphorical expressions in discourse, you simply assume certain de-contextualized metaphorical expressions and on the basis of those, you generate some kind of conceptual metaphor like ANGER IS FIRE. They suggest that if you want to be really systematic, you have to take a large corpora. By large, I mean really large. Probably they start with a 300 million-word corpora like the British National Corpus. They suggest that you have to look at a big corpus like that and identify all the particular metaphorical expressions that have to do with anger or all the fire-related expressions that have to do with anger, and then you can set up your metaphors and you can do whatever you like with them. They have as a goal to generate the complete list of metaphorical expressions and a complete list of conceptual metaphors in their methodology which goes against the intuitive selection of certain de-contextualized metaphorical expressions as it is assumed to be done by standard conceptual metaphor theory.

One of the main proponents of this view is Stefanowitsch, the German Cognitive Linguist who does corpus linguistics very well, and he says that we have to find all the metaphorical expressions for ANGER, for HAPPINESS, and so on. So he is one of the people who likes to attack my work. This is why I selected him as a good example of what the critics do—and he's extremely good at this. He looks at the British National Corpus and he finds thousands of metaphorical expressions for ANGER, for HAPPINESS, for SADNESS, and so on. Most of the metaphors that he finds are of an extremely general character. For example, he finds EMOTIONAL STATES ARE CONTAINERS, EMOTIONAL STATES ARE OBJECTS, CAUSES OF EMOTIONS ARE FORCES, EMOTIONAL CHANGE IS MOTION. Those of you who are familiar with "event structure metaphor" would immediately know that these are extremely generic level conceptual metaphors in what we call the event structure metaphor. Now he finds these, or he finds examples for these, by the thousands. He then says this is the only scientific and methodologically acceptable way of doing metaphor analysis.

I think there is a major problem with this kind of approach. The major problem is that we have to ask ourselves why do we have to find all these particular metaphorical expressions that are associated with particular target domains. Let it be ANGER, or HAPPINESS, or LIFE or THEORY or whatever. Is it the case that we have to find them because we want to generate complete lists of metaphors? Or is there a more worthwhile goal to do this? I think there is a more valued kind of goal that should be the purpose of doing metaphor analysis and doing metaphor analysis with the help of corpus linguistics. The idea is that we do this because we want to see how we use metaphors to conceptualize particular abstract concepts. It is not our goal to be exhaustive for the sake of being exhaustive. We do not want to generate complete lists, so that we can say ok, we found all the metaphors—all the metaphorical linguistic expressions for anger. No, the major goal of metaphor analysis should be to see how the metaphors that we find contribute to our understanding of concepts— abstract concepts like anger, like fear, like life and so on and so forth. In my view, this is a point that is missing from corpus linguistic studies of metaphor and I would like to encourage them to add this goal to their tool case, or to their conceptual purposes. That way I think they could make a really significant contribution to metaphor analysis and eventually (and essentially) to the understanding of abstract CONCEPTS in the conceptual system. So in a way I would like to see more collaboration between what I would call qualitative and quantitative approaches. This would be my particular way of combining the two.

The issue of schematicity has been observed by a large number of people that, there is some debate about whether Lakoff and Johnson and others place the metaphors that they come up with like THEORIES ARE BUILDINGS at the appropriate level of generalization or not. The reason why we have to worry about this is that depending on which level of generality you do your metaphor analysis, it can be important for being able to say why particular aspects of the source domain can be carried over to particular aspects of the target domain. You cannot make your metaphors too general because it turns out there are many things that you cannot carry over. You cannot make them too specific because in that case you will run into the problem that the metaphor will not allow for certain things that are carried over from source to target.

This was observed, for example, by Bill Croft here and you can read the quote. And they point out that Lakoff and Johnson place, for example, the THEORIES ARE BUILDINGS metaphor too high instead of making it more specific. They say that a convincing metaphor argument is like the physical integrity of a building—which should be or would be a better way of expressing or capturing the metaphor that Lakoff and Johnson wanted to capture.

So obviously, this indicates that there is a problem with the appropriate level of schematicity. I would like to look at another study, a study by Jörg Zinken, a German scholar, a metaphor scholar who looks at political discourse both in German and in English. So he is very much dedicated to a discourse-based, bottom-up kind of metaphor analysis. He is a key man doing metaphor analysis based on the natural discourse and his basic claim is that, in opposition to what most standard conceptual metaphor theorists claim that the mappings are at the superordinate level, he finds on the basis of natural discourse that they are at the basic level, that mappings instead of at the super-ordinate level, they are at the basic level. His argument is as follows:

> If they were on the superordinate level, the basic level concepts belonging to the same source domain that have similar meanings would merely be alternative manifestations of high level mappings and as such would have to be interchangeable, since the same mapping would apply to them.

So basically what he is saying is that if you have mappings at the superordinate level, and you have VEHICLE or CONTAINER at the superordinate level, then you will find certain manifestations of very high level image schemas, we can say, occurring in discourse in the form of basic level words. For CONTAINER you would find *kettle* and *pot*. And for PATH, you would find *course* and *way*. And for TRANSPORTATION, you would find *ship* and *boat*. His argument is that if mappings are at the superordinate level, then we should simply regard these as basic level manifestations of the superordinate image schemas and because they are manifestations of the same generic level image schema, they have to have the same meaning. They have to be applied in the same metaphors and they have to be interchangeable. What he finds is that they are not interchangeable and they don't have the same meaning.

Let's look at some of his examples. If you take *way* and *course* in German and English political discourse, and since both *way* and *course* are manifestations of the same superordinate level category or image schema, PATH, they have to be interchangeable in political discourse, but his argument is that they are not interchangeable; they mean very different things. So he says that the mappings in discourses are at the basic level rather than at the superordinate level.

Now it turns out that *way* is an example for the MEANS OF ACTION ARE PATHS metaphor, whereas *course* would be a part of the SCHEDULING HOW TO ACHIEVE ONE'S PURPOSE IS SCHEDULING HOW TO REACH ONE'S DESTINATION. This is my analysis. He simply points out that there are manifestations of the same superordinate category. They must mean the same thing, they must be interchangeable, they must be used in the same way in political discourse. He argues that they don't do it. They are not interchangeable, they don't mean the same thing. My argument is that they don't mean the same thing because, contrary to what he says, they are not a part of the same conceptual metaphor. They are completely different conceptual metaphors. So *way* is MEANS ARE PATHS, so we have to go this way and that way, that's the PATH, and you conceptualize MEANS OF ACTIONS. However, *course* is an example of a completely different conceptual metaphor, SCHEDULING HOW TO ACHIEVE ONE'S PURPOSE IS SCHEDULING HOW TO REACH ONE'S DESTINATION. In this way you can explain why they are different. So in other words, I do not accept that *way* and *course* are simply manifestations of the same superordinate category. There may be manifestations there, but they are at the same time examples of very different conceptual metaphors.

The other two concepts are *boat* and *ship*. He points out that in this case, they are a part of the examples of the TRANSPORTATION superordinate category. We use them basically for the same purpose—boats and ships. However, he points out that they are not interchangeable; they are used for very different purposes. The *boat* example is used when politicians talk about the need to cooperate, for example, by the way, you can find the same thing in English "we are in the same boat, so we need to cooperate with each other". And *ship* is primarily used in association with talking about the states or talking about the political party.

So they are not interchangeable either. You can make the same kind of argument for *kettle* and *pot*. So according to his reasoning, *pot* should be also a metaphorical manifestation of the CONTAINER metaphor, the HOT FLUID IN A CONTAINER metaphor, when we apply that to anger, because a pot is also a container, you boil water in it and so on. There is a major difference between the two and the main difference has to do with what I call the main meaning focus of the source domain. The main meaning focus of the source domain indicates the major function of a particular source domain. And the *kettle*, if we ask what the main meaning focus of *kettle* is, what we can suggest is that we use *kettle* as a source domain when we want to indicate some kind of emotional tension and we pick an item that exhibits the tension part, the pressure part, so we can have a metaphor something like EMOTIONAL TENSION IS PHYSICAL PRESSURE in the same way as there is pressure in the kettle. There is tension in the angry person emotionally.

If you compare this with *pot*, you find that *pot* behaves in a completely different way. A pot does not exhibit the same amount of pressure, hence the same amount of emotional tension that kettle does. So this is why we have *kettle* used in some cases for conceptualizing anger, while *pot* is not really used for that purpose.

The fourth issue is the issue of embodiment. This criticism maintains that Lakoff and Johnson—especially in *Philosophy in the Flesh* and later on, or together with Grady's theory of primary metaphor—place a huge amount of emphasis on universal aspects of embodiment. So you have the CONTAINER, and because this is universal, the metaphors that are based on this universal image schema will be universal. This is why in Chinese, in Japanese, in Hungarian, and in English, you have the same kind of generic level metaphor for anger: THE ANGRY PERSON IS A PRESSURIZED CONTAINER.

So the problem that people find with this is that if you think of embodiment, in a very naturalistic way, if you think of embodiment as a monolithic kind of thing, then you are running into problems in connection with your account of what is not universal about metaphor. We know that there is a lot that is not universal about metaphor. So the problem is how we can put together this monolithic conception as it is advocated by Lakoff and Johnson—this monolithic conception of embodiment with cultural and linguistic variation in metaphor and also in conceptual metaphor. Maria Rakova is the main critic here. She says "The thing is that reductionism and relativism are not supposed to go together. The failure to balance these two tendencies is, I believe, the second drawback of the philosophy of embodied realism." So what she finds problematic is that if you have a theory of metaphor—but probably you can think of not only conceptual metaphor theory, but more broadly for a theory of language and for a theory of the conceptual system—if you have a theory that is based entirely or mostly on embodiment which happens to be universal—and we have to admit that this is what Lakoff and Johnson and many others following them place a huge amount of emphasis on, then you run into all kinds of problems in accounting for obvious cases of non-universality in conceptual metaphors.

My way of handling this apparent contradiction is a relatively straightforward kind of conceptual tool that I call "differential experiential focus", "differential experiential focus". To see what this means, let me take the well-known example of ANGER and ANGER IS HEAT, ANGER IS FIRE metaphors, and say that ok, there are all kinds of physiological effects that seem to be going on when we are intensely angry: there is body heat, there is blood pressure, there is increasing respiration, and so on and so forth. We know this for a fact because there have been several physiologists and psychologists who actually did experiments like Paul Ekman to this effect and it indicates that we have all of these physiological responses in the association with intense cases of anger and it is this kind of embodiment that seems to explain the universal aspects.

For example, the ANGRY PERSON IS A PRESSURIZED CONTAINER metaphor. Now "differential experiential focus", as the name implies, would suggest that we should not regard embodiment as monolithic. We should regard embodiment as coming in different kinds of aspects, and different cultures and different periods may emphasize one aspect of these multiple forms of embodiment rather than another form of embodiment.

So a nice example I think is the ANGER IS HEAT metaphor because it seems to be applicable to English more easily than it is applicable to Chinese. On the basis of the work by Ning Yu, and some others like Bryan King, who did his dissertation on Chinese anger. His wife is Chinese, so I trust him. These people point out that somehow body heat plays less of a role in the embodiment of anger in Chinese than pressure does. Pressure seems to be more important in Chinese than heat, but in English and in Hungarian, at least in the contemporary context, you have both pressure and heat. You have both pressure and heat. If you move a little bit farther from Europe and China, and you go to the Ilongot tribe in New Guinea, you find that the Ilongot have a third way of basing their conception of anger. They think of anger as based on a generalized form of arousal, a generalized form of arousal which probably includes body heat, blood pressure, respiration, and so on so forth. So the generalized response is the most important thing for the Ilongot rather than just pressure or pressure and heat and so on. So my point is that we can explain some of the non-universality if we pay attention to the fact that embodiment is not monolithic. It comes in a variety of different forms and one culture and one language can pick out one aspect of embodiment and at the same time another culture might pick out another aspect of embodiment or you can generalize all of them in the form of arousal as is the case for Ilongot.

So we started out with a monolithic naturalistic conception of embodiment that characterizes Lakoff and Johnson and Grady, and then we moved on to "differential experiential focus" where we think of embodiment as having different aspects and each of the different aspects can be made use of in conceptualization. But now my suggestion is that not even this refined version of embodiment is sufficient for explaining many additional cases of non-universality.

In order to do that, I think we have to set up a principle that I call the "principle of coherence", the principle means that when we conceptualize anything and when we conceptualize particular abstractions in particular situations, then we seem to be under two kinds of pressure. One kind of pressure is the pressure of the body, that is, embodiment. The other kind of pressure that we have to somehow be aware of or pay attention to is context. And context, I will elaborate on what context is in later lectures. All I want to say now is that culture is one aspect of context but context is much broader than culture. So in an ideal situation, we want to be able to respond both to the pressure of embodiment and the pressure of context. There is some kind of competition in each and every situation, in which one wins out or one turns out to be stronger. Now this is an important issue because if you decide that all metaphors are based on bodily experiences, universal bodily experiences, then there is no way that you can explain all kinds of non-universality, there is no way that you can explain why in a particular situation, a particular conceptual metaphor is used rather than another.

Now let me very briefly give you a few examples of how this works in my mind. Let me give you an example that was used by Frank Boers, a Belgian scholar, although he just does not think of this in the terms that I do. This is my re-interpretation of his study. Frank Boers did a study of metaphors for economy. Over a ten-year period, he looked at the editorial articles in the British Weekly Journal Economist. He collected all the metaphors for that ten-year period. And he found something truly remarkable. What he found was that the ECONOMY IS HEALTH metaphor, which is a very common metaphor for economy—probably in China you also talk about a healthy economy, sick economy, and an economy that has to be revitalized, then what are the symptoms or whatever—so what he found was that the ECONOMY IS HEALTH metaphor is primarily used in the period between November and March.

And this was completely systematic for the ten-year period. He says, and I agree with him completely, this is because the period from November to March in Europe—probably in the western hemisphere but probably also here, because it seems to me that you have the same kind of seasons as we do—November to March would be the cold period; this is the period when people usually get colds, get bronchitis, get tonsillitis, get pneumonia, and so on and so forth. It's much more frequent than the summer period and than in spring period. So it seems to me that the physical environment can, in subtle ways, influence the metaphors that we choose for a particular target domain—in this case, ECONOMY. The physical environment is a part of the context. We are not thinking that oh, I am sick, now I will use the ECONOMY IS HEALTH metaphor. No, on a statistical basis, it seems to be the case that we are more likely to use the HEALTH metaphor in that period, rather than in other periods.

This was the introduction. I argue that as far as methodology is concerned, I think the opponents of standard conceptual metaphor theory make very valid points. However, there is a mix of different levels of the existence of metaphors here. As far as the direction of analysis is concerned, I find that if you use conceptual metaphor theory in more subtle ways, conceptual metaphor, higher level conceptual metaphors, mappings for those higher levels of conceptual metaphor, you can achieve more, a great deal more regularity than proponents of the bottom-up approach suggest.

As far as schematicity is concerned, you have to find the appropriate level of schematicity. One of the concepts that can help us with that is what I called the meaning focus of a particular metaphor as we saw in the case of *kettle* and *pot*. As far as embodiment is concerned, I think the criticism is partially valid and partially not valid. It is not valid because we can have a more sophisticated version of the embodiment hypothesis and the more sophisticated version is based on what I call differential experiential focus.

As far as how we can explain cultural variation, and as far as non-universality is concerned, I suggested that the pressure of universal embodiment and the pressure of local context are both at work at the same time and we try to obey and recognize both of these pressures in particular communicative situations.

Thank you!

LECTURE 2

Metaphorical Meaning Making: Discourse, Language, and Culture

Good afternoon! This is going to be the second introductory lecture before we go on to more serious and more detailed kinds of studies. The center of the approach that I'm using here is to study figurative language in relation to culture, and more generally, to context—and obviously the main notion is that of meaning. My claim here in connection with metaphor, language, and culture is that the common denominator to all of these things is meaning-making. That is, when we speak, it is an obvious case of making meaning with each other. But meaning-making is not limited to verbal communication. Meaning-making is taking place when in a particular context you are identifying people, you are identifying objects, you are identifying events. There's a great deal of meaning-making going on in all of these situations.

Also, meaning-making is happening when people behave. In general, when they behave, when they greet each other, when they hug each other, when they slap each other in the face, these are all kinds of meaning-making in the approach that I'm proposing.

Actually, this is not that weird of an approach to the relationship between language and culture and metaphor. This is something that can be connected to very distinguished theories in anthropology, and perhaps the most important person who also emphasizes meaning-making is the American anthropologist Clifford Geertz. You can see a definition of culture in his book *The Interpretation of Cultures* where he says, "Man is an animal suspended in webs of significance he himself has spun. I take culture to be those webs, and the analysis of it to be therefore not an experimental science in search of law but an interpretative one in search of meaning."

 All original audio-recordings and other supplementary material, such as any hand-outs and powerpoint presentations for the lecture series, have been made available online and are referenced via unique DOI numbers on the website www.figshare.com. They may be accessed via a QR code for the print version of this book. In the e-book, both the QR code and dynamic links are available, and can be accessed by a mouse-click.

As you will see tomorrow, I do not completely agree with this definition and I will discuss what it is that I do not agree with. However I very much agree with the first part of his definition of culture, "man is an animal suspended in webs of significance he himself has spun". This is very important for a cognitive linguist. This should be a very familiar kind of idea because after all, all Cognitive Linguistics is about is meaning. So Cognitive Linguistics, in my mind at least, is mostly about how people make meaning, whether by metaphor or non-metaphorical language, or constructions, or whatever.

Now according to this kind of definition, this would be a slightly different formulation of the same idea, culture is making sense together with other people. Notice that when we find examples, when we find situations that we cannot make sense of together with other people of the world, then we have cases of what are commonly referred to as "culture shock". In culture shock, what happens is that you interpret the role one way and someone else interprets the role in a completely different way. In this situation, you can't really understand each other and you cannot make meaning together.

So this is my basic approach to the notion of the relationship between language and culture, and this is what I am going to elaborate on today by way of some examples, and tomorrow, somewhat more theoretically by making use of all kinds of philosophical ideas about the nature of culture.

Now what is the most important organ that we have that has to do with meaning-making? Well it is the brain, and all the cognitive operations that run in the brain. We have this amazingly complex and valuable organ—the brain—and we have all kinds of cognitive operations running on it, cognitive operations like figure-ground alignment, metaphor, metonymy, conceptual integration, and many other things. The interesting thing about these, both the brain and cognitive operations, is that they are universal. However, the cognitive operations are not necessarily applied universally. We will see some instances when we have the same cognitive operations that we use to understand the world around us. It happens to be the case that members of different cultures do not use the same cognitive operations for conceptualizing the same areas of experience.

Now I don't like to suggest that this kind of approach is something that I invented. A very obvious predecessor is Geertz, as I mentioned. Also, in Cognitive Linguistics, several people have done similar things, although they did not necessarily conceive of this project in the same way and in the same terms as I do. The first person who did this was George Lakoff, in his discussion of American politics. He talked about American politics in terms of metaphorical conceptualization and in terms of framing and prototype categorization. Mark Turner also does something very similar in his 2002 book where he looks at a variety of cognitive sciences from the perspective of conceptual integration. I also do something very similar in my book *Metaphor and Culture* (2005), where I look at aspects of everyday culture. An anthropologist who very much adopts many of these Cognitive Linguistic ideas is Palmer, who actually invented a term that is commonly used for the same kind of enterprise that I am involved with here, and that is "cultural linguistics". So he is using the term cultural linguistics for discussing issues related to the relationship between language, culture, and cognition.

I want to look at some cases of non-metaphorical meaning-making. That will give us a nice contrast and will also highlight the point that we are making use of a variety of cognitive operations, not only metaphor and metonymy, and conceptual integration to understand both language and issues in culture.

The first example is spatial orientation. That is how people conceive of how things are related to each other and to the speaker in the world. The work that I want to say a little bit about is Levinson's idea, where he distinguishes between ego-centered spatial orientation systems and absolute systems. The important thing about this is that it shows that for a long time, linguists and anthropologists believed that spatial relations were conceptualized universally in the same way in all cultures, and the way they go about this is called ego-centered, the ego-centered way where you relate objects, spatially in the world in relation to your own body.

And so in English, for example, we talk about this thing to my right, to my left, and in front of me. You are in front of me, and the curtain is behind me, and so on and so forth. So here everything is related to the ego. This is why it's called ego-centered orientation.

Now, let's read the following passage about a completely different spatial orientation system as is described by Levinson. And these are his words. "Take, for example, the case of the Guugu Yimithirr speakers of North Queensland, who utilize a system of spatial conception and description which is fundamentally different from that of English-speakers. Instead of concepts of relativistic space, wherein one object is located by reference to demarcated regions projected out from other reference objects (ego, or some landmark) according to *its* orientation, Guugu Yimithirr speakers use a system of absolute orientation (similar to cardinal directions) which fixes absolute angles regardless of the orientation of the reference object. Instead of notions like 'in front of,' 'behind,' 'to the left of,' 'opposite,' etc., which concepts are encoded in the language, Guugu Yimithirr speakers must specify locations as (in rough English gloss) 'to the North of,' 'to the South of,' 'to the East of,' etc. The system is used at every level of scale, from millimeters to miles, for there is (effectively) no other system available in the language; there is simply no analogue of the Indo-European prepositional concepts."

So amazingly enough, when there is a fly buzzing in front of your nose, they do not say that "the fly is buzzing in front of my nose", they say "there is a fly buzzing to the north of me or the nose". I am not sure about the details. So this is a remarkably different system and it shows that what we take to be universally conceptualized are conceptualized as a matter-of-fact in a completely different way in this language. That is just a very powerful first example to show that different peoples, different cultures can go about conceptualizing the same thing in radically different ways.

Now here's a second example. Consider social debates. So here I would like to suggest that very often, social debates have to do with the structure of our categories. Now at this point it is important to give you a brief reminder of categorization in Cognitive Linguistics as opposed to the traditional view. As we all know, in the traditional view, categories are defined by necessary and sufficient conditions. There must be certain essential properties that hold categories together. As opposed to this, cognitive linguists and cognitive psychologists came up with the idea of prototype and claim that categorization is based on prototypes, so we have central members, non-central members, and so on and so forth.

My claim here is that in many cases, it is the nature of our categories that actually invites some social debates. When this is the case, we usually have that when debates are invited by the structure of our categories concerns what are called "contested categories". I could tautologically say that contested categories are categories that are debated in a particular culture. That is, categories people fight over—where they disagree about the definition of a particular category. Now, obviously "lamp" is not a contested category, although it can be contested. But typical contested categories are categories like "life". What is "life"?

Now philosophers and also everyday people can spend their entire lifetime trying to figure out what life is. The category of "love" is another contested category. The category of "freedom" is another one. What is "freedom"? George Lakoff wrote an entire book about this. I wrote a book on "love". I still don't know what "love" is. Many people have a completely different idea of it, like my wife that I divorced, unfortunately—apparently she must have had a very different idea about what love is. We disagreed.

My proposal here is that it is the very nature of our categories, namely that we have a prototype and we have non-prototypical cases that invite much of this kind of debate, and the particular example that I want to focus on is the category of "art", so like painting and music and literature and so on. The traditional conception of art, especially in the 19th and 20th centuries, we have art when there is some kind of symbolic representation of objective reality, like in a painting or a statue. We have a work of art when we have this symbolic representation, and it is representational, that is, there are figures like trees, people, landscapes, and so on, where we can identify all kinds of objects. So a work of art is typically representational in the traditional conception.

Thirdly, a work of art is some kind of physical object, some kind of physical object, like a painting, like a statue, and so on and so forth. Now I did a little study of 19th and early 20th century conceptions of art and the question is: are these necessary and sufficient conditions of art? Must they be present in order for us to be able to call something a piece of art, an object of art or not? Or we can ask the same question in terms of the prototype? Can we negate any of these features? Can we cancel any of these features of art? If you look at the history of art in the 19th century, it turns out that all of these three assumed or apparent criteria of art can be cancelled as a matter of fact.

So if you take that a work of art represents objective reality, this is not the case in several different forms of art. For example this is not the case in impressionism. As a matter of fact, impressionism denies that a work of art should be about reality as it is. It is your subjective impressions of reality that are important. So you know that it can be easily cancelled, and they said that our definition changes with this cancellation of an assumed criteria. A work of art is representational. That is, they must represent something. Now, in, for example, cubism and surrealism, that is not the case at all. Or abstract art where you have squares, and you don't really know what they are. There is a feature that was characteristic of the traditional conception and that is cancelled and successfully negated.

People who work or artists who work in, along the lines of either symbolism or cubism or surrealism said that, we don't believe that the traditional form of art is the way traditional-minded people define it. Interestingly enough, the third feature that a work of art is a physical object was also effectively cancelled by certain art movements in the early 20th century. There is something called conceptual art. In conceptual art, the main point is that a work of art is in your head. What you actually create in your head is what really matters, and there are all kinds of bizarre examples of this. My favorite is in the Museum of Modern Art in New York. I saw a chair standing against a wall. By the dictionary definition, this is a chair, and there is a picture behind it on the wall behind the chair. You know this is a very nice indication that a chair is a work of art, somewhere in the head, not simply in the physical object that we can see there.

METAPHORICAL MEANING MAKING: DISCOURSE, LANGUAGE, AND CULTURE   19

My point is that you have a traditional conception and the features that make up the traditional conception are successfully cancelled, and new definitions arise and these new definitions can arise because we have our contested categories structured the way they are, that is, they are structured by a particular prototype. The features of the prototype can be cancelled, and new definitions can emerge out of those cancellations. Now if we had categories that are defined by certain criteria, this would not be possible, then you could not cancel them successfully. You could try, but successfully you could not cancel any of these features. You can redefine art as we have seen in these examples, I would suggest that this is possible because of the structure, the prototype structure of our category of art.

The third example has to do with categorization and framing. And here what I want to say is that different individuals can interpret the same kind of reality in different ways. This is again well-known to cognitive linguists. We call this "alternative construal". We can apply different kinds of frames to the same piece of reality. Now, as a matter of fact, since frames represent categories, this whole issue is not only one of framing but also of categorization.

I want to give you an example where it becomes very clear that we are not forced to categorize things in exactly the same way but alternative construal is possible and we can use different kinds of categories and frames for the same aspect of reality.

Now consider a very everyday kind of example. Consider a hardware store. In a hardware store, you can buy nails. And what you find most often is that there are certain shelves where certain kinds of nails are kept. You will find, on shelves close to each other, long nails and short nails, and thin nails and thick nails, and nails with certain kinds of heads, nails without heads, wooden nails, and so on and so forth. So the point is that in the hardware store, and notice that this is not a linguistic example, this is an example in conceptual categories, the owner of the store or whoever arranged the nails, set up the shelves in such a way that the nails come together on the basis of some kind of similarity. This is a nice case of a non-linguistic form of "similarity-based categorization", or similarity-based categorization. The nails are kept together in this store very closely together because they bear some kind of "family resemblance" to each other.

Now, however, in the same store, let's assume they sell implements for hanging pictures on the wall. These may be in a completely different corner of this hardware store. You may find a wooden frame and maybe a ring, and maybe a hook on the frame and maybe a piece of string attached to the frame, and maybe a nail that you need to drive into the wall and then hang the frame with a picture in it.

Now the question is, how come this nail goes together with the wooden frame and the ring and the hook and so on? Why doesn't it go with the other nails? The reason why it doesn't go with the other nails in the other end of the store is that we have a different kind of categorization here. We have what we can call "frame-based categorization". So we can have both similarity-based categorization where items like the nails are together in one corner of the store because they resemble each other based on family resemblance. You can also have other kinds of nails in other parts of the store completely legitimately, I should say, because they belong to other groups—what they call "functional domains" or "frames", and we can make a basic distinction between frame-based and similarity-based categorization.

This is a non-metaphorical case of making sense of the world, but I like this example. I often send my students who are looking for a good topic for a term paper to go to all kinds of stores like hardware stores and supermarkets and do a report on why things are kept on shelves the way they are in particular stores. What lies behind all these is this kind of distinction.

Let me turn now to some examples of metaphorical meaning-making. The first thing I want to do is take the critics that I talked about in the morning seriously—those who suggest that cognitive conceptual metaphor theory researchers must use real discourse and base their analysis of metaphor on real discourse. I want to accept this kind of advice and look at certain cases of real discourse and metaphors in them and ask the question: what is the role of metaphor in real discourse. The most conspicuous role of metaphor in real discourse is to provide coherence to the discourse itself. I am not saying that this is the only role of metaphor, but a big role of metaphor in discourse is precisely this: to make discourse coherent. Let's address two kinds of coherence. I'm going to talk about what is called in post-modernist thinking "intertextuality" and "intratextuality".

I believe that intratextuality is closer to the heart of Cognitive Linguists but intertextuality is just as interesting and just as important because it raises the same issue of how we make sense of the world.

Two years ago I was in Durham, England, at what they call the Institute of Advanced Studies, and I had a very good time. Basically I had to do metaphor analysis, whatever I pleased to do. Durham is most famous for it's gothic cathedral from the 11th century. On my first excursion, I went to visit that church. This huge church is close to the institute. Now I went there and I got a book mark. The book mark had a prayer on it. I don't how many Christians there are in this room, or how much you know about Christianity. If you are not Christians or if you know nothing about Christianity, you will still understand what Christianity is all about based on this prayer. Ok, the prayer goes like this:

> Almighty God
> Who called your servant Cuthbert
> from keeping sheep to follow your son
> and to be shepherd of your people.
> Mercifully grant that we, following his
> example and caring for those who are lost,
> may bring them home to your fold.
> Through your son.
> Jesus Christ our Lord.
> Amen.

Now this is the prayer, and in order to understand the full significance of this, you need to understand a basic biblical story. This basic biblical story can be given in the set of mappings under the prayer where you have a shepherd corresponding to Jesus, the lost sheep corresponding to people who do not follow God, the fold of the sheep corresponds to the state of people following God, and the shepherd bringing back the sheep corresponding to Jesus saving people.

I'm not saying that this is all that Christianity is about, but this is one of the basic ideas. Now what does this have to do with intertextuality? Notice that this is a metaphor that is used in the Bible itself, in the New Testament. So we have that.

Now given that part of the Bible, this was used in the 6th and 7th century in England to ask Cuthbert who is mentioned here, "Almighty God who called your servant Cuthbert from keeping sheep to follow your son and to be the shepherd of your people", Cuthbert was a shepherd, importantly, and Cuthbert was asked to do the same thing that Jesus was supposed to do. That is, bringing people back to the fold. And in the 21st century, the priests in the Anglican Church in the cathedral are asked to do the same thing: bringing the people back to the fold.

Now what is nice about this, and this is where the intertextuality is, that in three very different historical periods, the same metaphor is used. But the values of the metaphor constantly change. First it is Jesus, then Cuthbert and then the priests in the Anglican Church today. So one metaphor is used throughout the ages with changing values to make sense of what we are, what human life is all about, at least in the Christian view.

Ok, now as I said maybe in intratextual coherence, not inter-textual coherence—that is, coherence within the same piece of discourse is perhaps closer to the heart of cognitive linguists who like to look at real discourse and analyze real discourse. So my second duty at the institute was to read the

London Times and analyze some of the metaphors that I found in it. And in one of the articles, this is what I found:

> Performance targets are identical to the puissance of the Horse of the Year Show. You know the one—the high-jump competition, where the poor, dumb horse is brought into the ring, asked to clear a massive red wall, and as a reward for its heroic effort is promptly brought back and asked to do it all over again, only higher.
>
> I've never felt anything but admiration for those puissance horses which, not so dumb at all, swiftly realize that the game is a bogey. Why on earth should they bother straining heart, sinew and bone to leap higher than their own heads, only to be required to jump even higher? And then possibly higher still.
>
> Hard work and willingness, ponders the clever horse as he chomps in the stable that night, clearly bring only punishment. And so next time he's asked to canter up to the big red wall, he plants his front feet in the ground and shakes his head, and says, what do you take me for—an idiot?
>
> Melanie Reid, The Times, Monday, February 4, 2008

This is a funny metaphor here and we can understand the metaphor if we look at the metaphorical mappings. Don't worry about the word "puissance", "puissance horse". I didn't know what that word meant either until I looked it up in a dictionary when I found the article. The puissance horse is the horse that is asked to jump obstacles in a Horse Show.

The whole article is about big companies and the relationship between workers in offices and their bosses. So what are the mappings? The puissance horses are the people who work for the big companies; riders are the managers; red walls corresponds to obstacles to the targets people have to achieve; having to jump over the obstacles—being subject to assessment; clearing the obstacles—achieving the targets; raising the obstacles—giving more difficult targets; the Horse Show corresponding to life.

So we have an article here that is about companies and how they function. More generally, it is about life and there is a symbol, a metaphorical analogy that we can call a conceptual metaphor that is set up between the Horse Show and the way large companies work. By understanding these mappings, we can make sense of the story in the newspaper article. This is what I mean by providing intratextual coherence.

Ok, now let me turn to another large issue of metaphorical meaning-making that has to do with universality and variation in metaphor. This is a large and complex issue. So let us just take a very small and simple example and ask the question of where do we find universality and where do we find non-universality in the use of metaphors? I talked about this a little bit in the morning, and now I want to suggest that when we look at metaphorical linguistic expressions, the chances are that we find a huge amount of non-universality. When we look at conceptual metaphors, the chances are that we find universality, but we also find non-universality.

Now consider one of the examples that Lakoff and Johnson very early on pointed out, and that is spending your time, which comes from the TIME IS MONEY metaphor, spending your time. Now "spending your time" in English has no [literal] equivalent in Hungarian. I don't know about Chinese. In Hungarian you cannot say that you are spending your time. What you can say is that you can fill your time. And that's quite different. That is based on a completely different metaphor. So when we look at metaphorical linguistic expressions, what we find is a huge amount of non-universality in addition to some universality. We can raise the question of whether non-universality is predominant or universality is predominant at the level of metaphorical linguistic expressions. This is a completely empirical question. I don't want to answer it—this is one of the things that corpus linguistic studies of metaphor could perhaps answer. So, my hunch is that when we look at metaphorical linguistic expressions in different languages, we will find a huge amount of variation.

However, as I said before, when we look at conceptual metaphors, the chances are much higher to find universal ones, and indeed these are the metaphors that cognitive linguists like to find. So let's look at the TIME IS SPACE metaphor—one of the favorite conceptual metaphors studied by cognitive linguists and anthropologists, because it is universal. There is evidence that it's found in English, Mandarin Chinese, Hindi, Sesotho. THE ANGER PERSON IS A PRESSURIZED CONTAINER can be found in perhaps dozens of completely unrelated languages. HAPPINESS IS UP is another universal metaphor that according to studies can be found in at least English, Chinese, and Hungarian.

The Event Structure Metaphor is a complex set of metaphors. So perhaps you would be somewhat hesitant to say that this is universal, but as Ning Yu shows, and as my studies indicate for Hungarian, English, Chinese, and Hungarian all have it. The KNOWING IS SEEING and the MIND IS THE BODY metaphor was pointed out to be almost universal, instead of entirely universal, but almost universal. This was pointed out by Eve Sweetser.

Now when we look at metaphors for our inner life, for example, in Lakoff and Johnson's *Philosophy in the Flesh*, what we found is SELF CONTROL IS OBJECT POSSESSION, SUBJECT AND SELF ARE ADVERSARIES, and THE SELF IS

A CHILD. This set of amazing metaphors for our inner life is shared by English, Japanese, and Hungarian. Maybe also Chinese could be shown to have it.

So the really significant question—and this is a question that was asked about 20 years ago by cognitive linguists and I think it was answered successfully by cognitive linguists—was that how is it possible that such complex sets of metaphors as the Event Structure Metaphor, which are extremely abstract, extremely hidden, extremely personal, and subjective would be universal for culture after culture? I should say that these are not absolute universals because there are about 5,000 different languages in the world, so I don't think we will ever find absolute universals as far as conceptual metaphors are concerned. But we can call them "near universal" if we find them in very distant languages.

So the question that was asked is how is it possible that there are so many at least near universal metaphors around the world? Essentially there are three possibilities to answer this question. You can say that by some miracle, by some lucky coincidence, it happens that you know dozens of unrelated languages have a particular conceptual metaphor. Another way to answer the question is to say that maybe you know one language borrowed it from another and another language borrowed it from the second and so on and so forth and it went around and it somehow became universal. I don't want to deny the possibility of this, but again the chances are that this is unlikely. It is especially unlikely if you go back several hundred years or if you go back thousands of years where you could find the same conceptual metaphors being universal. We could probably exclude the possibility that you know the Greeks borrowed something from the Chinese at the time or the Chinese from a non-existent English 2,000 years ago or 3,000 years ago.

There is the third possibility which is the most accepted for an answer to this question, and that is that these metaphors are universal because they are based on some universal bodily experience. This is the answer that is the favorite one in Cognitive Linguistic circles and I pointed it out in the morning that you know a refined version of this may be valid, but we need some refinements. Now, however, without any refinements, I just want to point out that, for example, the HAPPY IS UP metaphor can be found not only in English, but also in Chinese. These are examples taken from Ning Yu and also in Hungarian. The reason is that in most cultures when people are happy, they tend to be upward-oriented in many ways rather than downward-oriented, and so this is a pretty good universal bodily experience on which you can base this particular metaphor.

However we can move beyond this idea a little further. In my studies of emotion metaphors, I point out that the metonymies on which particular conceptual metaphors are based, can also be universal. As a matter of fact, the conceptual metonymies that seem to reflect some of the bodily responses can more readily be taken to be universal than the conceptual metaphors that are based on them. So the increase in BODY HEAT FOR ANGER kind of metonymy seems to be present in many cultures or languages. As a matter of fact, it seems to be present in languages that do not have the PRESSURIZED CONTAINER metaphor. So it looks like there is some kind of hierarchy here where you can have a metaphor, you can have a universally bodily base, and then you can have a metonymy based on it, and you can have a metaphor based on the metonymies. This is an interesting hypothesis that could perhaps be studied further.

Now another idea in the same direction was Joe Grady's notion of "primary metaphors" where he says that, for example, the THEORIES ARE BUILDINGS complex metaphor can be broken down into primary metaphors like LOGICAL ORGANIZATION IS PHYSICAL STRUCTURE. HAPPY IS UP is another primary metaphor, MORE IS UP, PURPOSES ARE DESTINATIONS, INTIMACY IS CLOSENESS, and so on and so forth. These are well-known. However, these are very local kind of metaphors. You have certain subjective experience and you have a correlation with some kind of physical experience in the body.

However, there seems to be a more global kind of universal metaphors, such as ANIMALS ARE HUMANS, HUMANS ARE ANIMALS, HUMAN ARE OBJECTS, OBJECTS ARE HUMANS, and so on. These are some of the metaphors that anthropologists like to study. One interesting study is by Keith Basso who points out in connection with the OBJECTS ARE HUMANS metaphor, that the Apache Indians, for example, conceptualize the car in terms of the human body. So the headlights are the eyes and so on and so forth. So this is a global kind of universal metaphor.

Now, however, given such global universal metaphors, there is the issue that although some of these global metaphors are universal, some others also have interesting non-universal variations to them. let's take the metaphor that spatial relations are parts of the human body. Now this is a metaphor that was worked on by Bernd Heine, a German cognitive linguist and anthropologist. He points out that although there is a universal tendency to see spatial relations in terms of the human body, it has interesting cultural variants.

One of them is that in some cultures, it is not the human body but the animal body that is important. Spatial relations can be structured by the animal body. The important question is, and this raises a new issue for us is why is it that a particular culture, or we can say perhaps particular tribes in the world, instead of using the human body as a source domain, use the animal body as a source for spatial relations. He suggests that this is the case where tribes and these people are close to nature and their major mode of subsistence is animal husbandry. They raise animals and they probably migrate with their animals, and live very close to them. They have a tendency to use the animal body for spatial relations.

Now that raises the following issue: given these universal tendencies that I was talking about before, when do we have cases where those universal tendencies don't seem to apply? What are the causes of metaphor variation? Cognitive linguists have found a very good answer to the question of what makes certain conceptual metaphors universal but they paid much less attention to the issue of what it is that produces conceptual metaphors. I want to suggest that there are essentially two causes involved in this. One is what I call "differential experience", and the other is "differential cognitive preferences".

Ok, let's start with differential experience. The most obvious way to talk about this is to observe that you get differential experiences when your social cultural context is different or very different from another group of people. Another one is when your social personal history is different from that of other people, or when you have different social or personal concerns from that of other people. Let me give you an example for each of these. So I mentioned that at the generic level—and I mentioned this example several times—you have the metaphor: THE ANGRY PERSON IS A PRESSURIZED CONTAINER. This is at a very high level of generality. If you look at this metaphor in different languages and cultures at a more specific level, what you find is that there are certain "key concepts" in the different cultures that seem to play a role and influence how you fill out this highly schematic metaphor.

So for example, in medieval Europe, THE ANGRY PERSON IS A PRESSURIZED CONTAINER was largely based on the theory of the four humors. We still have remnants of the theory of the four humors even today. However it has also changed a lot and we have the pressure cooker metaphor, the kettle boiling, and so on and so forth. However, in medieval times in Europe this was the main metaphor to use the theory of the four humors.

Now in contrast, in China, in Chinese culture, as you know much better than I do, there is the central concept of *qi* which I consider to be a key concept in Chinese civilization. The concept of *qi* plays a role in how you interpret or conceptualize THE ANGRY PERSON IS A PRESSURIZED CONTAINER metaphor. The pressurized container will be a human body that has *qi* running through it. When *qi* rises, you become angry and you can explode as a result, and you can spread the *qi* all over your body, and you can have a headache and a stomachache and all kinds of things. This is a fascinating topic also. The Chinese notion of *qi* provides an explanation for the Chinese way of conceptualizing anger. It also provides an explanation for all kinds of psychological and medical issues in this culture. My point is that if in medieval Europe, it was the theory of the four humors that kind of regulated the conception of anger, then in China, I don't know for how long, maybe for 5,000 years, it is the notion of *qi* that plays a key role in how the concept of anger is conceptualized.

Now there is this idea what I call "human concern". Human concern, what this is is that particular cultures and different individuals have different concerns, have different interests about the world. Some cultures are extremely dynamic and active; some other cultures can be said to be a lot more passive. Americans are said to be very dynamic and active. This is why they like sports and so on. Indians, on the other hand, are supposed to be passive. This seems to play a role in what their philosophies of life are and what their attitude to life is. If you pursue this idea, you can get some interesting non-universality in metaphor.

Antonio Barcelona, a Spanish cognitive linguist, came up with several ways in which sadness is conceptualized in all kinds of languages, including Spanish and English and Hungarian, SADNESS IS DOWN, SADNESS IS BURDEN, SADNESS IS DARK. All these make sense. They likely make sense to you as well. Maybe you conceptualize it in the same way. Now an extreme form of sadness is depression. So we would expect depression to be conceptualized in the same way as sadness is, and as a matter of fact, judging by some studies that were done by American psychologists, this is indeed the case with one very important exception. People with depression also conceptualize depression as being down, as being a burden, and being dark. However, they also conceptualize depression as being a captor, a captor that doesn't let you get free, doesn't let you get away, that keeps you in, that somehow puts a wall around you from which you cannot escape. The question is why did this particular metaphor emerge for depression? The simple answer is that it emerges because the most important concern of people who are depressed is how they can get rid of this condition, which is a terrible condition. For them, it's like experiencing being captured and being kept in and not being able to move freely in the world. This is why they developed this new way of understanding this extreme form of sadness that we call depression.

Ok, let me give you an example of how cognitive operations that are universal can be applied differentially in different cultures. So I mentioned in the morning that experiential focus explains why the Chinese take the pressure component in connection with anger as the basis of their metaphorical conceptualization of anger and that speakers of English take mostly body heat or a combination of body heat and pressure as their basis for conceptualizing anger. There is a difference in what they focus on. So this is what it means to have a different experiential focus. A more interesting case where you have, you apply differential cognitive operations to the same domain of experience is a case where in one culture you use a metaphor to conceptualize something and in another culture you use primarily metonymy to conceptualize the same thing.

A British cognitive linguist named Charteris Black looked at the concepts of mouth, tongue, and lip. Notice that these are speech organs. He looked at the metaphorical uses of these concepts in English and what he found was that there are many expressions in English that are used figuratively, either metaphorically or metonymically to understand and evaluate communication in general with these metaphors like "to be honey-tongued", and "to be tight-lipped".

Now he also looked at the figurative ways of understanding, figurative uses of mouth, tongue, and lips in Malay. What he found was something very interesting. He found that in Malay, these concepts of mouth, tongue, and lips are primarily used in metaphors as opposed to English where the expressions are primarily used as metonymies. He draws a very interesting conclusion from this. He says that this is because English as a culture is a more direct kind of culture, and metonymy is a more direct way of evaluating their communication than the more indirect metaphor would be.

And in Malay culture, it is very important not to hurt the ego of the person. It is very important to let your conversational partner keep their face. Face is very important and it is a terrible thing to hurt, to damage somebody's ego, reputation, face in that culture. And for this reason, although the same expressions can be used, there are a lot more metaphors based on these concepts in Malay than in English where it is predominantly the metonymies that are used. So here the point is that we can have universal cognitive operations. Both the Malay and English of course use metaphors and metonymy as cognitive operations. Certain social norms and social values can make one of these cognitive operations more important than the other, and this is why we find this fascinating difference between Malay and English in this respect.

Thank you!

LECTURE 3

Metaphor, Culture, and Embodiment

Yesterday I pretended to function as an anthropologist. Today I will pretend to function both as an anthropologist and as a philosopher. In the second half of my talk, we will have to get more serious about the exact nature of the relationship between metaphor, culture, and embodiment—this is the main issue for today. What is the exact nature of the relationship between metaphor, culture, and embodiment? In order to answer this question, I have to function again a little bit as an anthropologist and mostly as a philosopher, in addition to being a cognitive linguist.

Now yesterday when I was talking about the concept of culture, I mentioned that culture is essentially making meaning about the world and jointly making meaning with other people about the world and making meaning with them in more or less the same ways. Now I want to propose that we can take that kind of definition even further. Yesterday I was talking about everyday cases of how that kind of joint meaning making in the same way is happening when we understand what other people say, when we can make sense of other people's behavior, moreover, when we can identify objects and events in the world in the same way as other people.

However, we can take this definition of culture even further and say that this conception of meaning making can be found in the humanities. So not only on the level of everyday life but we can say that humanity is all about meaning making. I am assuming that most of you come from the English, or from the department of American studies. In general, I think that what people like us in the humanities are involved in is joint meaning making. Let me give you some examples of this joint meaning making in the humanities.

When literature scholars try to figure out what is going on in a novel or a poem, what their work is all about is making sense of the novel or the poem—they are looking for meaning. When many of us are engaged in, for example, the teaching of a foreign language, we are also engaged in the process of meaning

All original audio-recordings and other supplementary material, such as any hand-outs and powerpoint presentations for the lecture series, have been made available online and are referenced via unique DOI numbers on the website www.figshare.com. They may be accessed via a QR code for the print version of this book. In the e-book, both the QR code and dynamic links are available, and can be accessed by a mouse-click.

© ZOLTÁN KÖVECSES. REPRODUCED WITH KIND PERMISSION FROM THE AUTHOR BY KONINKLIJKE
BRILL NV, LEIDEN, 2020 | DOI:10.1163/9789004364905_004

making, we are trying to enable students to make meaning with others in a foreign language. When we study translation theory or when we actively function as translators, from one language to another, we are also engaged in meaning making. We are trying to make meaning available for speakers of other languages, other than the one that we are translating from. To a large extent, the work that we do in the humanities is all about meaning making. This notion of joint meaning making is crucial for the enterprise that I'm interested in, and this is why I have selected the definition of culture by Geertz as my leading idea into all of these issues. Because Geertz is the anthropologist who proposes—and you can find that his definition on the handout again—"Man is an animal suspended in webs of significance he himself has spun. I take culture to be those webs, and the analysis of it to be therefore not an experimental science in search of law but an interpretative one in search of meaning."

I chose this because this is an explicit formulation of culture as meaning making. However, the fact that I chose this as my starting point doesn't mean that I stop here and it doesn't mean that we do not have to go beyond this kind of definition. We as cognitive linguists are in a fortunate position to be able to go beyond this definition no matter how appealing this definition is.

There are two problems with this kind of definition by Geertz. One problem is that at the time when Geertz formulated his definition in the 1970s, we did not have sophisticated accounts of meaning making at that time. In the 1970s, Cognitive Linguistics, as we know it today, did not really exist. I propose that it is Cognitive Linguistics that can actually fulfill the Geertzian definition's promise. That is, when he talks about webs of significance, culture as webs of significance, and culture as being joint meaning making and culture as being an interpretive kind of enterprise. I think this kind of definition of culture can only be fulfilled with the means of Cognitive Linguistics. At the time when it was offered as a definition, when he actually defined culture this way, there was no available refined and sophisticated account of what meaning making was all about. We are in a fortunate position to provide that kind of account for how meaning making actually happens now. So that's one of the things that I would like to do throughout these lectures to talk about this more sophisticated kind of meaning making that we as cognitive linguists can perform.

The other problem, if you can call this a problem, with the Geertzian definition is that what he says in the second sentence, "I take culture to be those webs, and the analysis of it to be therefore not an experimental science". Now, I think this is another formulation, another aspect of the Geertzian formulation that we as cognitive linguists and cognitive scientists should not accept. We should say that the science of meaning making and the account of how meaning making is happening is very much an experimental science. Over the course of today's talk, I will give you one very clear and specific instance of why we need an account of meaning making along experimental lines when I talk about the particular set of experiments that relates very much to the issue of the relationship between metaphor, culture, and embodiment.

However, the main appeal to me of the Geertzian definition is that it allows us to think of culture as something non-monolithic—something that is kind of constructed, as webs of significance as he puts it, or constructed from society to society.

Now, so let me take up the first problem and let me elaborate on the issue of what would be a more refined kind of account of what meaning making is and how it is happening. In order to do that, we need to go back in time and we need to go back at least 50 or 60 years now and say that after the Second World War, there was a major cognitive revolution that is commonly referred to as the first cognitive revolution and the first cognitive revolution more or less coincides with a major discovery, with the discovery of the computer. And the main premise of the first cognitive revolution was that the mind is somehow like a computer and that is an analogy that was used at the time very much. Many of the people who participated in that revolution, like Chomsky, thought of the mind along those lines, and it is something that we still have today in a particular version of cognitive science.

In the late 1960s and in the 1970s there was a new revolution that we call the second cognitive revolution, which broke away from the premise that the mind should be imagined on the analogy of a computer. Instead, the new idea was that the mind, our main meaning making organ together with the brain, and its functioning is based on the human body—this is what we call "embodiment" today. Some of the people who explicitly recognize this include, for example, Eleanor Rosch in Berkeley, the cognitive psychologist whose work probably you know very well—especially her work on prototype categorization and basic level categorization.

Now given these two cognitive revolutions, there are two major camps that we can distinguish. George Lakoff and Mark Johnson make this distinction very clear and they talk about two ways of approaching how the mind works, two ways of approaching how we make sense of the world. The two camps are the "objectivist philosophy" or an "objectivist approach" to how we understand the world, and how we conceptualize the world, and the "experientialist" way of understanding the world.

I'll attempt to explain and characterize what these two ways of trying to understand the world are all about and how they differ in some major ways from each other. There are some major questions that these two approaches answer in very different ways. So when we ask what "thought" is, for example, we raise a number of issues: Is thought, thinking independent of the body? Is the mind transcendent? Is the mind abstract? Does it consist of the manipulation of abstract symbols, and is the mind like an abstract machine that is based on the computer analogy that I mentioned before where the mind is the software and the brain is the hardware. This would be one way of characterizing the objectivist approach to what the mind is and what thought is all about. In the experientialist mode of trying to understand the world, we would of course give a very different kind of answer to these questions and very different kind of characterization.

What about language and grammar? How should we think about language in the objectivist mode of philosophy, the objectivist mode of understanding the world? Should we think of language and grammar as a primarily form, as primarily highly structured form in the way for example Chomsky seems to think about language and grammar? Or instead should we think of language more in terms of meaning and conceptualization, as most cognitive linguists do?

There is a big question of what is meaning, and the two approaches to the conceptualization of the world, the nature of the conceptualization of the world give very different answers and raise very different issues. In the objectivist mode, meaning is a set of truth conditions, a set of necessary and sufficient conditions that have to be met as opposed to the experientialist way of thinking where meaning is a concept and you have an inner conceptual system.

There is another major question that addresses the nature of meaning in very different ways from the two approaches and that is: How do forms that we use become meaningful? When we use linguistic signs for purposes of communication, the question is: How do the forms that are a part of this acquire meaning, and how do they become meaningful? Do they become meaningful because there is simply some established kind of conventionalized relationships between the forms and an aspect of reality like objects and events? Or maybe the human body plays a role in imbuing those forms with meaning. These are some of the major questions that objectivist philosophy and experientialist philosophy answer in very different ways.

Meaning, of course, is the key term here and, that's why I am focusing on it, given the definition by Geertz and given the definition of culture as joint meaning making. In objectivist philosophy, for example, as I said meaning is defined by a set of necessary and sufficient conditions. If you take, for example, the concept, or the word *square* and you ask what is a square, you can define it as a geometric form that has four equal sides and four equal angles. This is the definition in terms of the necessary and sufficient conditions.

This is possible in some cases, but in most cases this is not possible. As we know in Cognitive Linguistics we would say that meanings are conceptual categories that are defined by a central member that we call the prototype, and all kinds of extensions from the prototype. And the symbols that we use, the forms that we use become meaningful as a result of our embodied experiences. Take, for example, the concept of a tree. Can we define the concept of a tree in terms of necessary and sufficient conditions? It doesn't make too much sense. However, if we ask what makes the concept of a tree meaningful, we can say that one of the things that makes a tree meaningful is a certain kind of embodied experience which is, for example, that a tree is tall. A tree is tall only compared to human beings. If we had very different kinds of bodies, we would probably not say that. If we were giants, let's say, then we would probably not characterize trees as being tall. But given the norms that we as human beings share, we understand trees as being tall. We also understand trees as being vertical probably because we also conceptualize ourselves as being vertical. So these are very clear embodied experiences of human beings that we project onto other things in the world. And because of this, we can say that the forms that we use become meaningful as a result of our embodied experiences.

Now given this way of talking about meaning, we can again provide the definition of culture and say that the culture is a large set of meanings shared by a group of people. This is a simple definition with all the things that I've mentioned so far included in it. Now this definition requires all kinds of things. It requires, for example, for people to have the organ of meaning making, the brain, the cognitive processes of meaning making, the body that makes linguistic and non-linguistic signs meaningful, and that imbues with meaning all objects and events that are not signs themselves like trees, for example, and the physical and social environment in which the brain and the body jointly evolve. So these are some of the requirements that have to be met in order for us to be able to talk about culture as meaning making.

In the experimentalist mode in Cognitive Linguistics, language is a set of linguistic signs, that is, pairings of form and meaning, and this is something that Bill Croft is talking about in his lectures. These are essentially constructions. It is very important to emphasize here that we have a shared set of such constructions, a shared set of linguistic signs, and because we have a shared set in a given culture, for a given linguistic community, this repository of meaning is extremely useful, is very useful for cultural purposes, because this conventionalized shared set of meanings provides us with a huge amount of stability over space and time.

Now, for this reason, if we think of culture this way, and we think of culture as a shared set of linguistic signs, we can understand the extreme importance of language in preserving particular cultures. This is why minority languages or dying languages, and speakers of these languages are so keen on maintaining their shared sets of linguistic signs. They want to, by keeping the language, keep their culture. This kind of definition of language is important for understanding what discourse is. We can think of discourse as particular assemblies of meanings concerning a particular subject matter. A special case of this is when we talk about ideologies. When we have ideologies, we put together certain meanings in a particular way that is important topics in a particular society at a particular time. So for example, the feminists have set up such a group of meanings and most of the debates about feminist issues are framed in terms of those meanings and this is what we can call an ideology.

Now, if we move on to the mind and if we move on to the issue of how we should think of human reason in this enterprise of trying to figure out the relationship between metaphor, culture, and embodiment, then maybe the most outstanding characteristic of human reason that stands out is that human reason is imaginative. Imaginative is understood in Cognitive Linguistics in a special way. It doesn't simply mean that it is poetic or creative. No, imaginative is used in a somewhat different sense in Cognitive Linguistics. It is used in the sense that whenever we can think of the world in alternative ways, we have to do with the imaginative character of human reason. Alternative construal basically comes about as a result of framing and metaphor.

Let me give you a nice example of how we get framing, or how we get alternative construal of the same aspect of experience by means of framing. There was an interesting study made by a psychologist among the Kpelle tribe in Africa. The experiment was about categorization and framing and there were four different things participating in the experiment. Hoe—and you know what a hoe is; you do that with the hoe—and knife, and orange, and potato. Now speakers of Kpelle, were asked to pair these concepts, and interestingly enough, the Kpelle, unlike the English, for example, set up the following two pairs, hoe with potato, and knife with orange. When Europeans did the same kind of experiment, they mostly paired orange with potato, because it's food, let's say, and knife with hoe because it's some kind of a tool they can use.

This kind of difference in framing between Europeans and the Kpelle is exactly the same kind of difference or is based on the same kind of difference that I talked about yesterday. I talked about similarity-based categorization and similarity-based framing as opposed to frame-based. Framing or categorization where you have a certain functional domain and you bring things together because they belong together functionally, so you use a knife to peel the orange but you use a hoe to hoe potatoes. So the funny part of the experiment was that the psychologist Joseph Glick who did the experiment asked the Kpelle, 'ok, how do you think a fool would pair these objects?' and the Kpelle said, ok, they would do it in the same way as the English do, that is, they would pair orange with potato and hoe with knife—that doesn't make any sense to us. So this is a nice example of how different cultures can go about framing in differential ways and obviously the Kpelle and most Europeans do it rather differently. That is an interesting instance of cross-cultural framing where different cultures solve the problem in different ways.

Metaphor is another major imaginative device of human reason that we can use to achieve alternative construal. I mentioned that in one view of metaphor, image schemas are extremely important. They provide the motivation for particular metaphors, so the CONTAINER schema, SOURCE-PATH-GOAL schema, the FORCE schema and so on, are all well known. SOURCE-PATH-GOAL seems to be the basis of the LIFE IS A JOURNEY metaphor; the EMOTIONS ARE OPPONENTS metaphor that I will be talking about this evening is based on the FORCE schema, and so on and so forth.

Grady's work on primary metaphor, where he points out that the level of something rising and adding more stuff to it, and the level rises. Primary metaphors are another instance where embodiment of some kind plays a role in and lies at the basis of particular conceptual metaphors. Now, I am mentioning this because it seems to me that there are essentially two strands of research in Cognitive Linguistics right now. In one there is a great deal of emphasis on embodiment and universality in metaphorical conceptualization. And in another there is more emphasis on context and variation. I am a representative of the second group. In most of my research, I am focusing on, in addition to issues of embodiment, the role of contexts in metaphor creation and on variation in metaphors.

Now, let me turn now to some further philosophical issues that are important for us in order to figure out the nature of the relationship between metaphor, culture, and embodiment. So I have emphasized alternative construal very much so far, and I have emphasized that because it is obviously a very important notion in, and characteristic of, Cognitive Linguistics.

However, it is not simply cognitive linguists who think of this relativistic, alternative mode of conceptualizing the world. There is a philosophical trend, a philosophical movement that very much thinks of our mode of understanding the world along similar lines and that is post-modernism. Post-modernist philosophers lay great stress on this relativistic conception of the world. So we find alternativity in understanding the world in Cognitive Linguistics, but we find alternativity as a highly emphasized notion in post-modernism philosophy, especially in one branch of it called social constructionism. Social constructionism is all about the unlimited, unbounded creation of different alternative ways of understanding the world. This alternativity fits very nicely with the Geertzian definition. To take this argument one step further, if there is all this alternativity that the cognitive linguists and post-modernist thinkers and philosophers emphasize, and if this is true that the human mind works in this way, the notion of embodiment that brings in issues of universality seems to be in conflict with this line of thinking.

If you emphasize social constructionism, the unbounded alternativity in ways of conceptualizing the world on the one hand, and embodiment that is universal leading to universality on the other hand, there are some conflicts. There are some conflicts here that need to be resolved, and I would like to talk about a way of resolving this issue. I would like to say that the notion of embodiment as a universalizing tendency should apparently be damaging to both the cognitive linguistic view of alternative construal, and it should be also damaging to social constructionism or post-modernist ideas of extreme relativity in conceptualizing the world. It turns out that it is more damaging to the post-modernist enterprise and in fact we will see that it is completely in line with the way cognitive linguists think about embodiment and alternative construal.

In order to find the resolution to this apparent conflict, I want to go back to the Geertzian definition again where Geertz says that this kind of interpretive science is not an experimental science. Now, I said at the beginning that I disagree with that part of the Geertzian definition and now I would like to show why I disagree with that definition. I would like to show that by giving you a fascinating experiment by an American cognitive psychologist Deniel Casasanto.

Deniel Casasanto takes the embodiment hypothesis very seriously and he says if the particular bodies we have play a role in how we normally represent abstract concepts—notice this is what we are proposing in Cognitive Linguistics—and results in particular abstract concepts, that is, the particular bodies result in particular abstract concepts, then different bodies should result in different abstract concepts. In other words, let me get ahead of myself a little bit and say what this means. If you have a particular body where you use your right hand, you are a right-handed, then this will have a certain impact on the way you represent certain categories related to this. You will represent them mentally, but if you are left-handed, you have a different kind of body in that sense, and that will result in a different mental representation of some of the categories related with this. We should find an example where this kind of embodiment has to do with a particular abstract concept. We do have one such concept—the notion of good and the notion of bad, these moral concepts. So he examined the GOOD IS RIGHT and the BAD IS LEFT metaphors. Of course BAD IS LEFT is just a hypothetical metaphor, however, GOOD IS RIGHT can be seen in several examples, in English and probably also in Chinese, for example when you say "he is my right hand man". You can say that in English.

Now he set up the following experiment. On the computer screen he had a cartoon figure and there were two boxes on the left and the right side of the cartoon figure. There were some good animals and bad animals that people had to sort in the following way. He gave them the instruction. He gave the subjects the instruction. Ok, the cartoon figure in the middle between the two boxes on his right and on his left likes the good animals but does not like the bad animals. Put the good animals in one box and put the bad animals in the other box.

Now what happened was that—and this is amazingly interesting—what happened was that the right-handed people obviously put the good animals in the right hand box, but the left-handed people put the good animals in the left hand box. Now notice why this is extremely important for us at this point. It is extremely important because of body specificity, that is what kind of body do I have in this sense plays a huge role in how you conceptualize moral concepts like good and bad. And left-handed people went along with their body specificity, right handed, and the results were around 70% in both groups. So the majority of people in the two groups went along with their handedness in assigning the animals to the two boxes.

Now this kind of result is presenting a challenge both to the possibility of unlimited alternativity in conceptualization and to the idea of unlimited constructionism. Now when I talked about this, when I talked about this to some post-modernism philosophers, they raised the following objection. Well, one of the things that you need to know about post-modernist philosophers is that they are completely relativistic, which means in our terms that they do not believe in anything like embodiment. Everything is social construction. Whether you are a man or a woman, it's a social construction. I would like to say that, there are certain signs of embodiment that make a difference, but not for them. So the objection that they raise was that, when you do this kind of experiment that Casasanto did, there is a huge amount of what they call cultural and historical baggage. There is a huge amount of cultural and historical baggage—that is, there are a lot more people who are right-handed than who are left-handed. This has become a cultural and historical convention. For that reason, it's very difficult to accept the results of this kind of experiment.

However, notice that two very different predictions are made in the experiment, cultural experiences should lead to good being associated with right, because conventionally the idioms of English, in the English language and culture made this manifest. So if you only base the thing on cultural experience, this is what should happen, and this should happen for both right-handers and left-handers, there are no idioms in English where GOOD IS LEFT. So, there is no conventional idiom in English or in any languages where good or moral is conceptualized as left. While physical experience should lead to good associated with rightwardness in the case of right-handers and left in the case of left-handers. So body specificity leads to specificity in conceptualization, so you can separate these two parts of the experiment very clearly and the results indicate that body specificity overrules or overrides or predominates over this assumed cultural baggage, cultural or historical baggage. If you are a left-hander, you will think of good as being left.

This is a beautiful example and this is a fantastic confirmation of the embodiment hypothesis in linguistics, and I use this experiment by Casasanto in many of my writings. Now, some of the work in Cognitive Linguistics that deals with the issue of embodiment is in need of repair, I think. One of the possible misconceptions about the issue of embodiment in Cognitive Linguistics is that it is conceived of in somewhat mechanical ways. To give you an example of why you cannot conceive of embodiment in a mechanical way, I'd like to tell you about another interesting study that was done on the history of English, and that was done on the ANGER IS HEAT metaphor.

One of the good things about corpus linguistics is that there are all kinds of collections now, not only of contemporary English and other languages but also we have historical documents turned into very usable databases in corpus linguistics, and you can study a particular concept given those historical databases for English and possibly for other languages as well. Now in one of these databases that is a collection of all the recent documents, for the English language beginning with the early middle ages, all the way up to the recent times, you can do searches on how anger was conceptualized in particular historical periods.

Now a Belgian scholar Caroline Gevaert did an interesting study of this that resulted in some very important pieces of information. She wanted to see the ANGER IS HEAT conceptual metaphor and in this historical database. What she found was that up until 850, the ANGER IS HEAT conceptualization for anger was very marginal. However, between 850 and 950, the conceptualization of anger in terms of heat became extremely productive. It went over 10% in the corpus. For some reason, after 950, it began to decrease. It went down to 6% and by the 13th century it was around 2% only. So what I mean by 2% is

METAPHOR, CULTURE, AND EMBODIMENT

that of all the expressions used for the conceptualization of ANGER, only 2% of them had to do with HEAT. Ok, and then, beginning with the 14th century, and this was about the same time when the four humors view that I mentioned yesterday came into being in Europe. The HEAT metaphors began to increase again, and we know the end result of that process, we have the HOT FLUID IN THE CONTAINER metaphor. Now, the same thing happened with the notion of PRESSURE, it also fluctuated.

Now this raises a very important issue concerning embodiment. If embodiment is conceived in a naturalistic and mechanical way, as it is done in most of the work in Cognitive Linguistics, then we are running into a major problem. The problem is this: if, for example, body heat is a universal and also historically valid property of heat and it should be because the human body didn't change through the ages; possibly people also produced body heat a thousand years ago in the same way they produce heat now, there is no change in that. If that is the case, then how is it possible that the percentages for heat throughout historical periods in English fluctuated. It should not happen. How is it possible that the idea of pressure also fluctuated in the different historical periods? It should not be happening.

Do you follow the argument? The human body didn't change, we basically have the same bodies we did a thousand years ago, five hundred years ago, and today. So if embodiment is taken in a mechanical way, if it is taken in a naturalistic way, then there is a conflict with this kind of fluctuation. Now this was another reason why I came up with the notion of experiential focus that I talked about yesterday, because if you think of anger as heat in terms of differential experiential focus, then you can say the following. Well, the concept of anger is conceptualized on the basis of a number of multiple physiological responses that are universal and that are preserved historically. It is not the case that in each and every historical period the exact same physiological response needs to be in focus. This is what experiential focus allows you to do, to shift focus on a particular physiological response rather than on another, or to another.

This is exactly what seems to be happening as a result of certain contextual factors. The experiential focus is shifted from heat to pressure, back to heat, and then a combination of heat with pressure resulting in what we have today—where we have in English at least, not in Chinese as I mentioned—where we have a combination of pressure and heat that leads to the kettle exploding. So we need a more refined version of embodiment.

Given all these things, let me turn to the major issue of the relationship between embodiment, metaphor, and culture. I mentioned yesterday that when we conceptualize something metaphorically, we are under two kinds of pressure, the pressure of the body and the pressure of the context. If we take, for example, the ANGRY PERSON IS A PRESSURIZED CONTAINER metaphor that I talked about yesterday, what we find is that this is a metaphor that is motivated both by the body and context. So the pressure of coherence must have worked when it was first used and it also works for us today. This is the idea that you have a conceptual metaphor that is based on both the pressure of the body and the pressure of context that I called body-based social constructionism. This is how we bring together post-modernist thinking with cognitive linguistic ideas.

This was the main conclusion of my book *Metaphor and Emotion*, where I introduced this notion of body-based social constructionism, primarily using the example of the ANGRY PERSON IS A PRESSURIZED CONTAINER. So that is a metaphor where we have an extremely strong motivation. Both the body and the context motivated the existence of that metaphor. So we saw this in the case of Chinese where it is the notion of "qi" that is the cultural input to otherwise universal bodily experience. Or we can take the notion of "hara" in Japanese, which is a key concept in Japanese culture that also fits into the metaphor and which makes it not only body-based but also culturally constructed.

These are perhaps the lucky the fortunate cases where we have this kind of double motivation for metaphors, both embodiment and context. In many other cases, however, it seems to be the case that the body predominates. One of the best examples of this is KNOWING IS SEEING.

We all know this metaphor; we know that there is a correlation between knowing something and seeing something. In this particular case we have the body predominating, we are under the pressure of the body, which predominates the motivation of the metaphor.

A very well known example of a conceptual metaphor that is predominantly motivated by a cultural basis is TIME IS MONEY. Lakoff and Johnson often use this metaphor to explain how certain cultural social conventions enter into setting up particular conceptual metaphors and this is a good example of that. The capitalist mode of production that correlates profit with time needed to make the profit is the case in point here. In another mode of production this metaphor is simply not known. But of course there is the process of globalization, especially today, so probably TIME IS MONEY is becoming a globalized metaphor and its way out the sphere of countries with a capitalist mode of production.

So in other words, I would like to conclude by saying that we have a gradient of motivation. We have a gradient where, at one end you have cases of conceptual metaphors that are predominantly bodily motivated, that's on the left-hand side. Right next to them, there are those cases where you have joint motivations that are motivated by both the body and some cultural factors, and that's what I call body-based social constructionism where cultures set up metaphors but also there is a combination with bodily motivation. Finally, on the right-hand side, there are metaphors that are predominantly based on cultural factors. This doesn't mean that when we talk about predominantly bodily motivation, there is nothing cultural. You shouldn't think that when we talk about predominantly cultural motivation, there is no bodily basis at all. My proposal instead is that we have a tinge of cultural motivation in the case of predominantly bodily-based metaphors, and we have a tinge of bodily motivation in the case of predominantly cultural metaphors. This is more faithful to the facts.

Now what about GOOD IS LEFT, the metaphor that was set up by left-handed people as an exceptional case. It is an exceptional case in the sense that it is a metaphor where body and culture are completely separated from each other. However, this is an exception that only reinforces the rule; in the majority of cases we have these two factors working jointly only in different degrees. There are no pure cases. And body and culture work jointly at all stages of the gradient.

LECTURE 4

Emotions I: A Cognitive Linguistic Theory

So as some of you may know, the major area of study that I have dealt with as a cognitive linguist is that of emotions. This evening and tomorrow morning I'm going to talk about my research on emotion concepts and especially on the role of metaphor in the conceptualization of emotions.

In my view, emotion concepts are composed of 4 different conceptual ingredients. The first one is metaphor, the second is metonymy, the third is what I call "related concept", and the fourth is cognitive models. These are the 4 ingredients that make up emotion concepts.

Now when I talk about emotions at conferences, and I tell people that I do not have a theory of emotions, everyone is surprised and disappointed. I have to repeat that claim here—I do not have a theory of emotions. What I have, what I do have, however, is a view of emotions that is based on the language of emotions. So I often refer to my own project as the "language of emotion" project, whose major result is the structure and content of emotion concepts.

I do not work like a psychologist who studies emotions. I do not work like an anthropologist who studies emotions. I do not work like a philosopher who studies emotions. I do not want to give you a new theory of emotions. I want to give a theory that is built into and based on language, and that is going to be a "folk theory" as opposed to an "expert theory" of emotions. It is not an expert theory in the way in which Darwin, for example, had a theory of emotion or in the way psychologists have particular theories of emotions. This is a folk theory which is based on the language we use to talk about emotions. I study the way we talk about the emotions, then on the basis of that discourse, I try to find out what the major ingredients are.

I'll start with metaphors. I will give you two sets of examples just to indicate some of the similarities and some of the differences between metaphors for anger and metaphors for love. So probably, the ANGER metaphors are well known to you. We have the HOT FLUID metaphor, the FIRE metaphor,

All original audio-recordings and other supplementary material, such as any hand-outs and powerpoint presentations for the lecture series, have been made available online and are referenced via unique DOI numbers on the website www.figshare.com. They may be accessed via a QR code for the print version of this book. In the e-book, both the QR code and dynamic links are available, and can be accessed by a mouse-click.

© ZOLTÁN KÖVECSES. REPRODUCED WITH KIND PERMISSION FROM THE AUTHOR BY KONINKLIJKE
BRILL NV, LEIDEN, 2020 | DOI:10.1163/9789004364905_005

the INSANITY metaphor, the OPPONENT metaphor, the CAPTIVE ANIMAL metaphor, the BURDEN metaphor, the NATURAL FORCE metaphor, SOCIAL SUPERIOR metaphor, and so on and so forth.

Now if we look at the concept of love, what we find is that LOVE is conceptualized as a NUTRIENT. It is JOURNEY. Maybe the most common metaphor is the UNITY metaphor, LOVE IS A UNITY OF TWO PARTS, "we're *as one*", or "they're *breaking up*", or "we're *inseparable*" or "we *fused together*." LOVE IS A BOND. LOVE IS A FLUID IN A CONTAINER; LOVE IS FIRE; LOVE IS AN ECONOMIC EXCHANGE—that one is very important, "I'm putting more into this relationship than you are", a very commonly heard complaint. LOVE IS A NATURAL FORCE, "she swept me of my feet". LOVE IS A PHYSICAL FORCE. You can be drawn to someone. LOVE IS AN OPPONENT interestingly. You sometimes, for all kinds of reasons, have to try to fight your feelings of love. LOVE IS A CAPTIVE ANIMAL; LOVE IS WAR; LOVE IS INSANITY; LOVE IS A SOCIAL SUPERIOR. She's completely governed—ruled by love. LOVE IS A RAPTURE OR A HIGH. You can be high on love or drunk on love. The object of love is conceptualized in all kinds of ways.

Now as you can see, some of the metaphors for LOVE, and some of the metaphors for ANGER are the same. They are the same in the sense that the source domains are the same. So we find in ANGER, the FIRE metaphor, we find that for LOVE. We find the OPPONENT metaphor, and we also find that for LOVE. We find the NATURAL FORCE metaphor for ANGER; we also find that for LOVE. These are very interesting similarities and you'll see in a minute why I find them very interesting and very important as an observation of the structure of emotion concepts in the field of emotions in general.

Now the second main ingredient of emotion concepts is metonymy. Let me take LOVE, and let me look at some of the metonymies in connection with LOVE. You have probably experienced many of these, and maybe some of them are culture specific, but I think all of them make sense to you, and you will probably not be terribly surprised that these are metonymies for LOVE. INCREASE IN BODY HEAT STANDS FOR LOVE, "I *felt hot all over* when I saw her" is very common experience. Or INCREASE IN HEART RATE STANDS FOR LOVE, "he is a *heart-throb*". So this is an expression that is commonly mentioned, for example, in connection with Brad Pitt. Because he is so good looking, and women go crazy about him, and he makes their hearts throb. "He is a *heart-throb*". BLUSHING STANDS FOR LOVE, DIZZINESS STANDS FOR LOVE. You can be in a daze; you can feel dizzy every time you see someone. SWEATY PALMS, very common. INABILITY TO BREATHE STANDS FOR LOVE, "you *take my breath away*". There is a very famous popular song, "you take my breath away"—some of you may know it. INTERFERENCE WITH ACCURATE PERCEPTION

STANDS FOR LOVE, "he saw *nothing but her*". You have this kind of tunnel vision. PHYSICAL CLOSENESS, INABILITY TO THINK STANDS FOR LOVE, "he *can't think straight* when around her". PHYSICAL CLOSENESS STANDS FOR LOVE, "they are *always together*". INTIMATE SEXUAL BEHAVIOR STANDS FOR LOVE: "she *showered* him *with kisses*", "he *caressed* her *gently*". SEX STANDS FOR LOVE, "they *made love*". A short comment on this, notice that I am not saying the word *love* is used metonymically here. What I say is that "make love" is a euphemism for sex, and *sex* is used metonymically for *love*. I am not saying this is a logical inference that you can make, that when two people have sex they are in love, but this is a possibility.

It is a possibility for you to make the inference, when you hear that two people made love/engaged in sex that they maybe love each other, but it is not necessarily the case all the time, of course. LOVING VISUAL BEHAVIOR STANDS FOR LOVE, "he can't *take his eyes off her*", "she is *starry-eyed*", and so on and so forth. So this is a rich set of metonymies that indicates the most important physiological behavioral and expressive reactions that people produce, conventionally, when they are in love with each other.

There is also related concepts ingredient. By related concepts, I mean those emotional attitudes or emotions that are involved in another emotion, that is you have emotion A, and emotion A assumes that presence of emotions B, C, D, E, and so on and so forth. So if we relativize these to romantic love, romantic love, not every kind of love, but romantic love, then you can legitimately assume that if two people say that they are romantically in love with each other, then you can make the inference that they like each other; they feel sexual desire for each other; they are intimate with each other; they long for each other; they feel affection for each other; they care for each other; they respect each other; and they consider themselves to be friends with each other.

Note that this gives a pretty natural explanation for why in English, two people who are in love are called 'boyfriend' and 'girlfriend'. This is the explanation and we can say that related concepts more or less function like metonymies. Another minor note that I want to add here is that we will see that the structure of emotion concepts is extremely complicated. For centuries and certainly in the 20th century, philosophers have loved to study love for some reason. The way they tried to find love was in terms of such necessary and sufficient conditions as these related concepts here, "liking", "desire", "intimacy", "longing", "affection", and so on and so forth. Then, they fought with each other about what the criterial features are, and which are the ones that can be left out, and so on and so forth. This is a much bigger topic that I cannot go into here.

Now, given these three, I will get to the fourth major element a little bit later. But at this stage of the analysis, we can ask a major question: Is there what we can call a "master metaphor" for emotions? That is, is there a generic level metaphor that somehow subsumes most of the metaphors that we have seen so far? As you will see in a minute, my answer to this is 'yes'—there is such a generic level master metaphor. I identified this master metaphor with the help of Len Talmy's "force-dynamics". When I read his paper called "force-dynamics", which is a paper written in 1988, that's when I started to work on the idea that maybe there is a more general metaphor here, which can be captured and described with the help of "force-dynamics". We have a 'force-dynamics' situation when there are two entities in interaction with each other, and they affect each other. Now there are force entities: there is an "agonist" and "antagonist". There are intrinsic force tendencies that characterize the agonist and antagonist, there are two of them, either "toward action", or "toward rest". There is what he calls "resultant of the force interaction" and it can be either "action" or "rest", or "inaction" and there can also be a "balance of strengths"—the stronger and weaker entities can balance each other.

Now the most skeletal structure of emotions is the following. There is a cause that leads to an emotion. Then in the second step, the emotion leads to some response. My claim is that this kind of skeletal structure is based on two applications of what we call the CAUSES ARE FORCES metaphor. And the CAUSES ARE FORCES metaphor is the metaphor that comes from the Event Structure Metaphor, and it is well known.

So what I would like to do now is take particular generic level emotion metaphors like EMOTIONS ARE OPPONENTS and analyze them in terms of "force-dynamics" in the way Talmy describes it.

Let's take the OPPONENT metaphor, and here are some examples: you can be *seized* by emotion; you can *struggle with* your emotions; you can be *gripped*; you can be *overcome by* emotion, and so on. Let's consider EMOTION IS AN OPPONENT and try to lay it out according to Talmy's "force-dynamics" pattern. In the source domain you have Opponent 1 and Opponent 2, and then you have a resultant action at the source domain level. Opponent 1 corresponds to the agonist; Opponent 2 corresponds to the antagonist. We can ask, what is the force tendency of Opponent 1? Well, in this particular metaphor, Opponent 1's force tendency is to attempt to resist Opponent 2. Opponent 1 and Opponent 2 are in interaction such that Opponent 1 is kind of *gripped, overcome, seized*, and so on. As a result, either Opponent 2 or Opponent 1 wins. Opponent 1 wins when there is no effect—they do not change.

Now at the target level what we find is that the agonist or the entity that corresponds to Opponent 1 in the source domain is the "rational self". Rational self attempts to try to maintain control. The rational self doesn't want to lose control. The emotion, however, which functions as the force here, causes the self to lose control. In the case of most emotions and many real world emotional situations, what happens is that the self loses control. It can also happen, of course, not prototypically that the self maintains control.

Now notice that this particular table and this particular configuration of entities in interaction is based on the second part of the skeletal scenario. We already have emotion in existence. The emotion is affecting a more or less passive Opponent 1 be able to maintain control over emotion or give in to the force emotion? The same applies to the NATURAL FORCE metaphor.

So what happens in the case of NATURAL FORCES—like floods, winds, and so on? You have a physical object, and the physical object is just standing there, staying the same. There is a natural force affecting it, causing an effect in the physical object, or, metaphorically speaking, attempting to cause an effect in the physical object. Similarly, what you find is that the rational self tries to continue to behave as before the emotion. The emotion is causing the self to respond to the emotion, and the self responds to the emotion in a passive way.

Notice that the phrase "in a passive way" is very important, because that's the main meaning's focus, as I would say, of the NATURAL FORCE metaphor when we apply the NATURAL FORCE metaphor in general, not only in the case of emotions, but especially in the case of emotions. What is suggested is that anything that is affected by an extremely strong powerful natural force will passively undergo certain changes.

Now the first part of the previous emotion scenario or skeletal scenario is captured by the EMOTION IS A PHYSICAL FORCE metaphor. Physical force can be a mechanical force—perhaps physical contact. So, for example, "when I found out, it *hit* me hard"; "this was a terrible *blow*"; "she *knocked* me *off* my feet". I imagine the situation that you are just standing there, and all of a sudden, you see this beautiful woman, and you say "she *knocked* me *off* my feet". This is a situation in which the beautiful woman would be the cause of your emotion. We can analyze the situation using terminology borrowed by Talmy. The physical object remains unaffected by the force—that's the force tendency of the physical object. However, the force tendency of the antagonist is to produce an effect on the object. The force tendency before I see this beautiful woman, is to remain unemotional, but then there is an effect that comes from the cause of emotion, and it causes the self to become emotional. So as the result: self becomes emotional—angry, happy, sad, in love, and so on and so forth.

Now all of these things lead us to a much richer model of what emotions are like, what emotion concepts are like, what the cognitive model of emotions is, and of what emotions in general may be like. What we find is that there are four steps here. This is both a temporal and causal kind of order. This characterizes the typical emotional situation. I repeat the typical, the prototypical, the paradigmatic, and the central case of this emotion. It doesn't mean that in each and every emotional situation this is what happens.

Step one is the cause of emotion. The cause of emotion has a certain force tendency. There is the rational self, and the rational self has a certain force tendency, and force tendency of the cause and the force tendency of the rational self are in conflict. In a typical emotional situation the force tendency of the cause tends to be stronger—the cause overcomes the defenses of the rational self, and as a result the self now has emotion. The self has a certain force tendency now, and there is another force tendency of the emotion and the two are in conflict. The force tendency of emotion is to make the self elicit certain effects, and produce certain responses. Eventually the self does produce the appropriate emotional responses. I say "appropriate" because each and every emotion requires different emotional responses, or sets of emotional responses.

This is a general characterization of emotion concepts in terms of a generic level schematic cognitive model that I have laid out here. Now we can go on to the next question, which is: Are emotion metaphors unique to the emotions? In a way, at the beginning I suggested that they are not, at least some of the major ones are not. The question is which ones are unique to emotions, and which ones are not unique to emotions. If you look at the very general EMOTION IS A FORCE metaphor—this is very schematic metaphor—it assumes all kinds of metaphorical source domains for emotions like the PRESSURIZED CONTAINER, OPPONENT, NATURAL FORCE, BURDEN, and so on. These are all specific level instances of the schematic EMOTION IS A FORCE metaphor. And so we can ask: Are these metaphors unique to emotions or not? If you look at language, what we find is that these particular specific level emotion source domains are not unique at all to the emotions.

For example, the PRESSURIZED CONTAINER metaphor can be used in the following instances, you can talk about trouble *brewing* somewhere, or you can talk about the situation being *explosive*. These are not necessarily emotion situations. So the application of these specific emotion source domains is not really limited to the emotion domain, but goes beyond it. If we similarly look at the OPPONENT metaphor, you can *struggle with* your emotions, but you can also *struggle with* differential equations; you can *struggle with* mathematics; and you can *struggle with* many other things. So the OPPONENT source domain is not limited in any way to the concept of emotion.

As a matter of fact, if we take this argument further, what we find is that in the case of morality, we find the same metaphors. What is morality? Morality is a situation where there is some kind of temptation like a cause, and the cause is making an effect on you, and the cause is influencing you, but you successfully resist the force of that cause, of that temptation. For example, let's say I am the last person to leave this room this evening, and I find a bag with one million US dollars in it. I would be tempted to keep it. It would put a certain force on me to go along with the cause, and keep the one million dollars. But if I am moral, I will successfully overcome the force. That is, my rational self will turn out to be stronger than the desire to keep the money. So what happens in this case is that morality and emotion are very similar events at this very generic level structure with one exception. The exception is in the case of emotion you give in to the cause, you give in to the force and cause overcomes you. In the case of successful cases of morality, the cause doesn't overcome you. You manage to resist this.

Now let's see some of the conceptual metaphors that seem to be unique to the emotions. Well, there is TRESPASSING and PHYSICAL ANNOYANCE for ANGER. There is a very famous American metaphor "to bug someone", to irritate someone. That is a PHYSICAL ANNOYANCE, and so a generalization of that is PHYSICAL ANNOYANCE when someone is bugging you. That is some kind of physical annoyance. So ANGER is PHYSICAL ANNOYANCE, and ANGER is TRESPASSING—"I *draw the line* here."

There is a HIDDEN ENEMY, SUPERNATURAL BEING METAPHOR for FEAR—you can be *haunted* by something in English. Your fear can haunt you, or a particular object or idea can haunt you—that's characteristic of FEAR. BEING OFF THE GROUND, AN ANIMAL THAT LIVES WELL, PLEASURABLE PHYSICAL SENSATION for HAPPINESS. When you are walking on air, for example, I don't know whether you can say that in Chinese for HAPPINESS. That is an example that I have in mind. And HAVING NO CLOTHES ON and DECREASING SIZE and BLOCKING OUT THE WORLD for SHAME. Ok, in American English, people often say things like "I felt completely naked", meaning I felt extremely ashamed or embarrassed. And for DECREASING SIZE, I have noticed that some Americans like to gesture that and they say "I felt this small", and "I wanted to disappear from the surface of the earth", and so on and so forth.

So, now, the question that I would like to raise here is what makes these particular metaphors, conceptual metaphors, unique to the emotions as opposed to the previous sets of cases that seem to be very general and extend over the domain of emotions, and also characterizing all of the emotions, or most of the emotions, not just some of them. These ones seem to be unique to particular emotions. DECREASING SIZE or HAVING NO CLOTHES ON for SHAME are unique to SHAME. They don't apply to FEAR, they don't apply to HAPPINESS or ANGER. I would like to suggest that these are unique to particular emotions, because they are based on either the cause of that particular emotion, or the effect of a particular emotion.

So if you look at ANGER IS TRESPASSING, ANGER IS A PHYSICAL ANNOYANCE, FEAR IS A HIDDEN ENEMY, FEAR IS A SUPERNATURAL BEING, A HAPPY PERSON IS AN ANIMAL THAT LIVES WELL, HAPPINESS IS A PLEASURABLE PHYSICAL SENSATION. These are all metaphors whose source domain is based on the cause of the respective emotions. So TRESPASSING, for example, or PHYSICAL ANNOYANCE, these can be actual causes of ANGER, but they are, so to speak, elevated to the status of a source domain for ANGER as well, and become conceptual metaphors. So we have ANGER conceptualized in terms of one of these causes.

The same applies to HAPPINESS, PLEASURABLE PHYSICAL SENSATION. "I was *tickled pink*", tickling is a pleasurable physical sensation. We can take it to be one of the causes of happiness, and given that, it can be generalized and turned into a source domain of HAPPINESS, and HAPPINESS, as a result, can be conceptualized.

SHAME IS HAVING NO CLOTHES ON is one of the major causes of feeling ashamed. When you are caught having no clothes on, you are ashamed, but this can also be generalized. The cause of shame can be turned into one of the source domains of SHAME. We also find the same thing in connection with the effect of emotions. For example, SHAME IS A DECREASE IN SIZE is based on one of the potential behavioral effects of shame. When you are ashamed, we often would like to disappear, and it is turned into a source domain. My prediction would be that those metaphors for particular emotions that are based on unique responses, either causes or effects, can become metaphors or source domains to conceptualize those emotions.

How do emotion metaphors differ from metaphors for relationships? By relationships, I simply mean human relationships—perhaps friendship, marriage, or love. We can ask whether we have the same kind of structure for relationship concepts that we have for EMOTION concepts. We can ask whether something is similar to the EMOTION IS FORCE metaphor, which is a high level schematic metaphor subsuming several specific level metaphors—do we have a situation like that for personal relationships like friendship, marriage, and love? In order to answer this question, I looked at the concept of FRIENDSHIP in English on the basis of some questionnaires, and self-descriptions of instances of examples of *friendship* by native speakers of American English. It turned out to be the case that friendship in English, at least for my American subjects, seems to be based on 6 very different metaphor systems.

The six metaphor systems on which the American understanding of friendship is based, include what I call the communication system. So I found metaphors like COMMUNICATION IN FRIENDSHIP IS SHARING OBJECTS. So people often talk about how wonderful it is to share their experiences with their friends. So this is what it meant by this one. Also the metaphor system for emotions was involved to some extent, I should say, to a very small extent, especially in the form of two metaphors, EMOTIONAL INTENSITY IS TEMPERATURE and EMOTIONAL CLOSENESS IS PHYSICAL CLOSENESS. EMOTIONAL INTENSITY IS TEMPERATURE, either warm or cold.

So "our friendship is getting *colder* these days" or something like that. EMOTIONAL CLOSENESS IS PHYSICAL CLOSENESS, "we are *close* friends". States and Relationships, STATES ARE OBJECTS, as we know from the Event Structure Metaphor. RELATIONSHIPS ARE BONDS, so "there is a strong *bond* between my friend and I". INTERACTIVE RELATIONSHIPS ARE ECONOMIC EXCHANGES. This is very common, especially for love and marriage, not so common for friendship. An example of this would be the one that I mentioned at the beginning of the lecture, which is "I am putting more into our friendship than you are". This can be used for romantic love, and also for marriage. What I call the "metaphor system for complex systems" is also involved. ABSTRACT COMPLEX SYSTEMS ARE BUILDINGS and MACHINES and so on. So people often say that they would like to "*build* a good friendship", and "their friendship is somehow not *functioning*, or not *working* with a particular person".

The Event Structure Metaphor characterizes, I mean the metaphor system for events characterizes friendship just a little bit, because friendship is taking place in the context of life. So I find certain instances of the LIFE IS A JOURNEY metaphor. The last one is the metaphor system for positive and negative evaluation. So people often talk about how valuable their friendship is for them. This is what I call the DESIRABLE ENTITIES ARE VALUABLE THINGS metaphor.

Romantic love is a special case—everyone notices that love is extremely metaphorically conceptualized, and now we know why it is so highly metaphorical. Well, it is highly metaphorical, because it assumes all the metaphors of emotions and all the metaphors of relationships. The nature of love is such that it is at the same time an emotion and a relationship. It takes the metaphorical source domains from both of these, so SHARING OBJECTS, DISTANCE, WARMTH, BOND, ECONOMIC EXCHANGE, BUILDING, IMPLEMENT, MACHINE, PLANT, JOURNEY, VALUABLE COMMODITY, and so on.

So do we find a master metaphor for relationships in the same way as we found the master metaphor for emotions? I would say no. The only thing that we can find is certain statistical evidence that seems to indicate that there are two groups of metaphor that are statistically more productive than the others that stand out in their productivity. These are the metaphors that we can take to characterize interactive relationships. By interaction I do not simply mean the ECONOMIC EXCHANGE metaphor, but also sharing experiences where there is some interaction going on in terms of what two people experience. So that's one set of metaphors that is characteristic of relationships. Another set of metaphors is what I call the COMPLEX ABSTRACT SYSTEMS. As I pointed out in the first lecture, the COMPLEX ABSTRACT SYSTEMS metaphor consists of the BUILDING metaphor, the IMPLEMENT metaphor, the MACHINE metaphor, and the PLANT metaphor. All of these have specific meaning foci that may be used of and taken advantage of by FRIENDSHIP, which is some kind of COMPLEX ABSTRACT SYSTEM, and also MARRIAGE and LOVE.

So there is a big difference between the structure of human relationships, the metaphorical structure of human relationships, and the metaphorical structure of emotions. The most important difference, it seems to me, is that in the case of emotions, we have a single hierarchical structure where you have EMOTION IS FORCE, a very schematic metaphor, and underneath it, you have more specific source domains, and underneath that still more specific ones, and so on and so forth. We do not seem to find this in the case of friendship. In the case of friendship what we find is that there are at least 6 different metaphor systems that show a hierarchical arrangement. So that is a very interesting kind of difference in my mind, because it tells us that when we try to envisage what the conceptual system might look like—you have relationships and you have emotions, you will think that they have to be structured more or less the same way, but they seem to be very differently structured.

Let's turn back to the emotions and let's ask the next question which is: what is the role of metaphors in the cognitive construction of particular emotion concepts? I will go through this very briefly because this is well known stuff from my work with George Lakoff where we describe the concept of ANGER and our major point is that all the conceptual metaphors and metonymies that we have for ANGER contribute to a particular cognitive model of ANGER. We make use of those conceptual metaphors and the mappings of those conceptual metaphors to construct a particular cognitive model of ANGER—anger coming into existence, the attempt to control it, loss of control, retribution and anger's intensity.

What is more interesting, however, is when we try to compare this cognitive model of ANGER that is based on the metaphors and metonymies that we found for English with cognitive models that are based on other languages. Bryan King proposed that in Chinese, when I say in Chinese, if you have an offending event, anger comes into existence, attempt at control, release of anger, release of anger, and restoration of equilibrium. Now you can see that the difference—sometimes slightly different or very different conceptual metaphors—that you find in Chinese like the "qi" metaphor and the way the "qi" metaphor, excess "qi" in the body and what it does and how it functions does make its contribution to the cognitive model. It changes the cognitive model in comparison to English. As a matter of fact, King goes further and he suggests that in Chinese there is an additional cognitive model that is different from the first in the last two stages of the model, there is diversion and there is a compensating event.

So I think this is how far a cognitive linguist can go. When you look at the language and you look at all the metaphors that you find in a particular language, you put together the cognitive model on the basis of the mappings that you find in those conceptual metaphors that are available. From there, your job ceases as a cognitive linguist, and you have to ask people whose job it should be to decide to what extent the models that are based on emotion language in English, emotion language in Chinese, Hungarian, and so on, are actually working in those particular languages. So I don't know what your intuitions are, but we probably would need experimental psychologists who would do large scale surveys among native speakers of Chinese and native speakers of English to see whether these models actually exist in the heads of speakers of these languages.

If you try to generalize again on the basis of such detailed, specific emotion scenarios, or models, you can come up with a slightly different skeletal models than the one I showed you previously. We can observe that there are three parts that must be there and that are likely to be there in any model based on, more than likely, any language—that is these models have an ontological component, a causal component, and an expressive component. Now the expressive component may or may not include a control element. Notice that this is purely a case of social conventions—how much a particular emotion is controlled or regulated in a particular society is an issue that can be built into the cognitive models and this is why you can have this kind of schematic model: 1. cause, existence of anger, or 2. its counterpart in the form of force, 3. attempt at control; 4. loss of control, and expression.

The question is how metaphors can create such a model, and, well, this is a tricky issue—and there are two major camps here. There are people who claim that these metaphors don't actually create the models, they simply reflect preexisting models, but of course then the question would be: How did those preexisting models come into existence? I don't want to go into this, this is a huge topic, and this is still an unsettled debate. In my view, most of the emotions—at least the basic emotions—are characterized by one or several of what I would call "major emotion metaphors".

By "major emotion metaphors", I mean the ones that are capable of creating such structures as we have seen here. They create at least the skeleton of these structures that we have seen here and the PRESSURIZED CONTAINER metaphor for ANGER is one such model for English. That metaphor can be laid out, the mappings of that metaphor that can be laid out in the container with the substance corresponds to the person who is angry, the heat and the pressure of the substance corresponds to intensity, forceful substance in the container to anger, and so on and so forth—this is very important in the case of English.

However I am not suggesting that this is universally the case. For example, in Zulu, according to work by Taylor, it seems to be the case that the NATURAL FORCE metaphor and the HUNGER metaphor for anger are much more important for the construction of the Zulu model of ANGER than the ANGRY PERSON IS A PRESSURIZED CONTAINER metaphor is.

Now again just a side note, it is not accidental that Sigmund Freud in the early 20th century set up a model of emotions that we call a "hydraulic model" of emotions. The hydraulic model of emotions is very similar to what the ANGRY PERSON IS A PRESSURIZED CONTAINER metaphor describes. You have a force inside a person or the repressed things and those repressed things want to come out of you, you try to control them but there is an explosion and so on and so forth. So Freud's version of psychoanalysis can be derived, or traced back at least, to this language-based folk conception of how the emotions work and especially the way ANGER works.

LECTURE 5

Emotions II: Life and Happiness

We have seen that many examples are based on the conceptualization of emotions are based on universal bodily experiences, so then can we expect any non-universality in emotion concepts? So, you understand what the issue is. The issue is that, if when we are emotional, we are producing the same kind of physiological behavioral expressive responses all over the world, then there is the inevitable question of whether we can have non-universality, whether we can have variation and a large amount of variation at that concerning emotion concepts. So this is the theoretical background to the topic of sexuality that I briefly want to discuss here.

I want to look at a particular metaphor that was discovered in several completely unrelated languages. In English, it is very common to talk about sexuality, especially sexual desire or lust, in terms of heat and you will find some of the examples of this, in your handout: "she's *burning* with desire"; "I've got the *hots* for her"; "he's *on fire* for her", and so on and so forth—there are many such metaphors. In a completely unrelated language, such as Hungarian, you find the same kind of metaphor, and when you look at this metaphor, SEXUAL DESIRE IS HEAT or SEXUALITY IS HEAT, and given these examples that I have just given you, we can have the following set of mappings between the source and the target. The thing that is hot from the fire corresponds to the lustful person. The heat corresponds to lust, that is to the sexual desire itself. The degree of the heat corresponds to the intensity of the lustful feeling. So when you are hot, it may not be as intense, your sexual desire may not be as intense as when you are on fire. When you are blazing, for example, that's a very high degree of intensity.

Now, in an African language, a completely unrelated third language, Chagga, which was studied by Michelle Emanatian, the LUST IS HEAT metaphor is interestingly different. Notice that we have lust, or sexual desire, we have heat in the source domain, so on the surface this conceptual metaphor looks exactly

All original audio-recordings and other supplementary material, such as any hand-outs and powerpoint presentations for the lecture series, have been made available online and are referenced via unique DOI numbers on the website www.figshare.com. They may be accessed via a QR code for the print version of this book. In the e-book, both the QR code and dynamic links are available, and can be accessed by a mouse-click.

© ZOLTÁN KÖVECSES. REPRODUCED WITH KIND PERMISSION FROM THE AUTHOR BY KONINKLIJKE BRILL NV, LEIDEN, 2020 | DOI:10.1163/9789004364905_006

the same as earlier mentioned metaphors. But as we will see, there are subtle variations in the Chagga application of this metaphor in comparison to the English and the Hungarian version.

So these are some of the examples that I take from Emanatian's work. Unfortunately I can't reproduce the Chagga version of this, but you can say "she *burns*" or when you say "she has a *heaven of fire*" in the literal translation, that in fact means she has desirable sexual qualities. When you say "she is cold", what that means is that she lacks desirable sexual attributes. So the Chagga heat metaphor for sexuality works in a somewhat different way from English and Hungarian. If we take these examples as representative examples in Chagga, and that's all we can do, we get a somewhat different set of mappings to characterize this metaphor.

So the thing or the substance burning corresponds to the woman with desirable sexual qualities. The warmth or heat of the thing or substance corresponds to desirable sexual qualities of a person. The person who observes the burning thing corresponds to the man who finds a woman sexually desirable and attractive.

So notice what is happening here, what is remarkable about the Chagga way of conceptualizing sexuality is that first of all, the metaphor is used from the perspective of men only. These are all examples that are used by men. Notice that these are examples from the perspective of a man who finds a woman desirable and it is the sexual desirability of the woman that is conceptualized in terms of heat.

So this is very different from the English version where it is either the man or the woman. The intensity of the sexual feelings are conceptualized as heat. Here it is the desirability or the sexual attractiveness of the woman from the perspective of a man. So the way I think about this is to say that there is a re-conceptualization—there is a re-framing here of both the source domain and the target domain in comparison to English. But of course, there are certain indications that English can do the same thing. For example, if you say of a woman, "oh, she is hot', that would be very close to the Chagga application of the metaphor from the perspective of a man talking about the desirable sexual qualities of the woman. But you cannot say, unlike Chagga, that "she is on fire" or "she is burning" and mean she has very desirable sexual qualities.

However, the adjective *hot* seems to have the same kind of duality in terms of the two frames that we see as the difference between Chagga and English. Maybe I would talk with Bill about this whether he agrees or not about *hot* being used in both of these ways.

We can draw a very important conclusion from this. We can have basically the same conceptual metaphor that is motivated by the same physiological responses. Sexual desire produces an increase in body heat, and that is characteristic of both Chagga and English, and possibly also Chinese and Hungarian. Unlike English, Chagga reframes both the source domain and the target domain when they apply this particular metaphor. That indicates what we mean when we say that, we can explain conceptual metaphors, the universality of some conceptual metaphors because they have the same bodily motivation. This is not quite a sophisticated or subtle way of putting the issue because there can be further interesting re-framings or re-conceptualizations between the conceptual metaphor and the bodily motivation.

At this point, I want to talk about happiness in particular. So in this particular lecture, instead of talking about emotion concepts in general, and talking about all kinds of theoretical issues in connection with the emotions, I want to focus my attention on the concept of HAPPINESS. I also want to look at the concept of LIFE and eventually I want to show that the conceptualization of the concept of LIFE is intimately tied with our conceptualization of HAPPINESS.

Let's look at the conceptual structure of the concept of HAPPINESS in English. As I mentioned yesterday, all emotion concepts, at least the basic ones, have four major conceptual ingredients: conceptual metaphors, conceptual metonymies, related concepts, and particular cognitive models, as representations of these particular emotions.

So let's first see the conceptual metaphors of HAPPINESS as they can be recovered from the language that is used about happiness in English. However, instead of talking about HAPPINESS metaphors globally I think we should distinguish three different types of HAPPINESS metaphors. There are certain HAPPINESS metaphors that we can call "general emotion metaphors". These are metaphors that we saw for the characterization of emotion concepts in general.

So HAPPINESS takes its own share of most of those metaphors that we saw yesterday. So for example, we have HAPPINESS IS A FLUID IN A CONTAINER, "she was *bursting with* joy"; HAPPINESS IS HEAT/FIRE, "*fires* of joy were *kindled* by the birth of her son". Most of these examples come either from internet searches or from dictionaries. HAPPINESS IS A NATURAL FORCE, "I was *overwhelmed* by joy." Or you can even be "*hit* by happiness" if happiness comes unexpectedly and suddenly, you can say that. You can even be "*seized* by joy" as in the OPPONENT metaphor. Even the CAPTIVE ANIMAL metaphor can be used, and I found this on the internet: "all joy *broke loose* as the kids opened their presents." HAPPINESS IS INSANITY, "the crowd *went crazy* with joy"; HAPPINESS IS A FORCE DISLOCATING THE SELF, "he was *beside himself* with joy". Here, a normal person is inside a container but when you have intense feelings of joy you can be beside yourself. HAPPINESS IS A DISEASE, "her good mood was *contagious*". These are very general HAPPINESS metaphors and these are shared, or at least most of them are shared with most other basic emotion concepts.

Now, the next set of happiness metaphors can be characterized as those metaphors that provide some kind of evaluation for the concept of HAPPINESS. As we could expect, the major way to evaluate happiness is that it is a very positive kind of state. So we have HAPPINESS IS LIGHT, "he was *beaming* with joy"; HAPPINESS IS FEELING LIGHT (not HEAVY), "I was *floating*"; HAPPINESS IS UP, "I'm feeling *up*"; HAPPINESS IS BEING IN HEAVEN, "I was in *seventh heaven*".

The third group of HAPPINESS metaphors is different. These are metaphors that provide what we can call a phenomenological character for the concept of HAPPINESS. What this means is that they provide a feeling tone, kind of, for what happiness is like. HAPPINESS IS AN ANIMAL THAT LIVES WELL, "I was *purring* with delight", you can say that. HAPPINESS IS A PLEASURABLE PHYSICAL SENSATION, "I was *tickled pink*". HAPPINESS IS BEING DRUNK, "it was an *intoxicating* experience"; HAPPINESS IS VITALITY, "he was full of *pep*"—pep is an informal, slangish term meaning full of life or vitality. HAPPINESS IS WARMTH, "what she said made me feel *warm* all over". So these are all metaphors that seem to describe the way you feel when you are happy. This is why I call them phenomenological metaphors for HAPPINESS.

Let's look at the conceptual metonymies of HAPPINESS. The conceptual metonymies of HAPPINESS indicate the major responses that people produce when they are intensely happy. The responses that people produce when they are happy can be classified into three groups: we can have behavioral reactions or responses, physiological responses, and expressive responses. The behavioral responses are well known: JUMPING UP AND DOWN FOR HAPPINESS. When I say JUMPING UP AND DOWN FOR HAPPINESS, I want to indicate with the word FOR that there is a "stand for" kind of relationship, a metonymic relationship. So you can "jump up and down with joy". You can have something like "dance with joy", dancing, singing, and so on. Other behaviors can also stand for happiness. So if you see people doing this, you can probably make the inference that those people are happy.

Physiological responses: FLUSHING FOR HAPPINESS, you can "flush or beam with joy"; INCREASED HEART RATE FOR HAPPINESS, your heart beats faster and faster, something like that with joy; BODY WARMTH FOR HAPPINESS, "be *warm* with joy". AGITATION/EXCITEMENT FOR HAPPINESS, "be *excited* with joy". There are also expressive responses that can be displayed on the human face. These are primarily the responses that people like Paul

Ekman study when they look at basic emotions on the human face. There is also BRIGHT EYES FOR HAPPINESS—you can "shine with happiness or joy"; and SMILING FOR HAPPINESS, this is of course a major kind of conceptual metonymy for happiness. This doesn't mean that every time that people smile, they are happy, but again it is a completely legitimate inference that when you see someone smile, the chances are that they are happy. That may not apply when you are in China or Japan, and it also doesn't mean that every time you see a person smile, the person must be happy—but the prototypical kind of association is that when you are happy, you smile.

I talked about this yesterday in connection with LOVE and now we can see how they characterize HAPPINESS. There is the issue of SATISFACTION. If you are happy, it can be assumed that you are satisfied with something. There is a goal you want to achieve, you achieve it, you are satisfied, and then you are happy. PLEASURE, not in the sense of sexual pleasure, of course, but this minor feeling of pleasure—you can do something with pleasure. You do something happily, or with joy. FEELING HARMONY, and when we are happy, we as if we are in harmony with the world. So these are general characteristics of HAPPINESS, as regards related concepts, conceptual metonymies, and conceptual metaphors.

Now, given all these conceptual ingredients of metaphors that we took one by one, it is possible to build a cognitive model for HAPPINESS. As a matter of fact, it is possible to build three distinct cognitive models for HAPPINESS that we can take to be the central cases of happiness—the prototypes of happiness. The first one, I call "happiness is an immediate response". This is a very intense form of happiness. It is an intense form of happiness when you achieve something that is difficult to achieve; when you achieve it, it makes you extremely happy. Given the metaphors, the metonymies, and the related concepts, we can characterize this form of happiness with the following cognitive model. "Happiness is an immediate response" is usually expressed in English interestingly not with the word *happiness* but with the word *joy*.

This is the "joy prototype of happiness". So there is "the cause of joy". You want to achieve something; you achieve it. There is an immediate emotional response to this on your part. "The existence of joy"—you are satisfied, you display a variety of expressive and behavioral responses including brightness of the eyes, smiling, laughing, jumping up and down, and so on. You feel energized—this comes from the VITALITY metaphor. You also experience physiological responses, including body warmth and agitation/excitement.

The context for this state is commonly a social one involving celebrations. This is a form of happiness that you don't get inside your own room. This is something you experience when you go out to celebrate a major achievement. You feel a need to communicate your feelings to others. The feeling you have may "spread" to others. This is the "contagious part". You experience your state as a pleasurable one—you feel that you are in harmony with the world. You can't help what you feel. You are passive in relation to it. The intensity of your feelings and experiences is like a high. Beyond a certain limit, an increase in intensity implies a social danger for you to become dysfunctional, that is, to lose control. It is not entirely acceptable for you to communicate and give free expression to what you feel (i.e. to lose control).

Now this is extremely culture-dependent. Some cultures make it more difficult. Some other cultures make it easier for people to express the way they experience happiness. So depending on your social contexts and depending on your society or culture, because it is not entirely acceptable to communicate and/or give free expression of what you feel in some cultures, you try to keep the emotion under control. We have all these OPPONENT metaphors even in HAPPINESS. You attempt not to engage in the behavioral responses and not to display the expressive responses or not to communicate what you feel. Of course, in the prototypical scenario, you lose control, and you engage in behavioral responses and display expressive responses or communicate what you feel. You may, in addition, exhibit wild, uncontrolled behavior, often in the form of dancing, singing, and energetic behavior with a lot of movement. As I said at the beginning, this is a very intense form of, this is a very salient form of happiness. As we will see, this is not the only form of happiness. There are other forms of happiness.

Again, there is the issue of how we get this particular cognitive model. How do we get them on the basis of the metaphors, metonymies, and related concepts? A large part of the way we get this model comes from the mappings that characterize the particular metaphors and metonymies of that we have seen. So for example, there are certain metaphors like the NATURAL FORCE metaphor, the OPPONENT metaphor, the CAPTIVE ANIMAL metaphor, and the INSANITY metaphor. In connection with HAPPINESS, all seem to indicate that there is some kind of loss of control in, as the final stage of the experience of happiness. Again this is only possible and only happens when you have a very intense form of happiness—an extremely salient kinds of happiness.

The other much more subdued form of happiness is what I would call "happiness is a value". "Happiness is a value" is characterized by a number of conceptual metaphors like HAPPINESS IS LIGHT, HAPPINESS IS FEELING LIGHT (NOT HEAVY), HAPPINESS IS UP, HAPPINESS IS BEING IN HEAVEN, and very importantly, HAPPINESS IS A HIDDEN DESIRED OBJECT. Ok, you can say "at long last I have *found* happiness".

The first four of these metaphors are especially about providing an evaluation for the concept and experience of happiness. Obviously all these metaphors provide very positive evaluations for it. We can perhaps characterize "happiness is a value"—this form of happiness is actually referred to with the word *happiness* and not with the word *joy*. What we find in this case is that we can assume that there are some major purposes or goals in life like (freedom), (health), (wealth), (love), and so on that serve as the causes. I put them in parenthesis because these are not particular goals and purposes that you actually set yourself. This is not like "I want to be an Olympic champion" and then you become an Olympic champion. These are just assumed desires in most societies by people. We all want to be free, we all want to be healthy, we all want to be wealthy, and we all want to find love.

Now there are certain actions that we perform and the actions that we perform are encapsulated, so to speak, in the HAPPINESS IS A DESIRED OBJECT metaphor. The action is that of searching. The action is that of trying to find the major values and eventually be satisfied and living in harmony with the world. Now this searching action is difficult, this is why one of the features in this part of the model is "it is difficult to obtain". You have to look for it. You have to pursue it. It requires effort to obtain it. It takes a long time to obtain it. Once people obtain it, however, it lasts a long time. The "desired result" part of the model is when you achieve your goal and you are free, you are wealthy, you find your love, and so on and so forth. In that case, happiness is associated with very positive values—happiness is pleasurable, happiness gives you a feeling of harmony with the world.

This cognitive model of HAPPINESS is very, very different from the first one. As a matter of fact, there's also a third one that I call "happiness is being glad", but I do not talk about it here. I have a fairly old paper from 1991 where I described the three cognitive models for HAPPINESS based on English: "happiness is an immediate response", that's what we talked about a minute ago; "happiness is a value"; and "happiness is being glad".

Now, I mentioned that the "happiness is an immediate response" kind of model is usually not referred to by the word *happiness*. It is referred to by the word *joy*. It is the second "happiness is a value" model that it commonly referred to as happiness. We can ask whether this is just, a subjective judgment on my part or we can find some evidence for this and it turns out that several years after I wrote that paper in 1991 and I made that claim on the basis of my own intuitions and intuitive judgment. There were two studies from two completely different fields of study that seem to confirm this notion that the first one is "joy", the second one is "happiness". One of these was a study by Stefanowitsch based on his work in corpus linguistics. He looked at all the metaphorical and metonymic expressions and he found that the distinction that I draw between "happiness is an immediate response" and "happiness is a value" is also reflected in the use of particular words in English, *happiness* and *joy*, referring to the two kinds of models that I mention. So corpus linguistic studies seem to confirm that kind of claim. Also, there was a study by Tseng, Hu, Han, and Burgen who are cognitive psychologists and linguists, and they also seem to have come to the same conclusion.

Let me turn to the concept of LIFE. The concept of LIFE is one of the most celebrated concepts in metaphor studies for very good reasons. There are at least two reasons. It is a prototypical abstract concept and also it is, as I mentioned yesterday or the day before yesterday, a contested concept. There are many different ways of understanding what life is and I try to collect most of the metaphors that provide a particular way of looking at what life is.

LIFE IS A JOURNEY is a stock example in cognitive metaphor theory. LIFE IS A BUILDING; LIFE IS A MACHINE; LIFE IS A PLAY. I am taking all of these conceptual metaphors for life partly from my work and partly from Lakoff and Turner's work *More Than Cool Reason*. LIFE IS A PLAY; LIFE IS A PRECIOUS POSSESSION; LIFE IS A STORY was made famous by Shakespeare, for example, "life is a story told by an idiot signifying nothing". LIFE IS FIRE; LIFE IS LIGHT; A LIFETIME IS A DAY; A LIFETIME IS A YEAR; LIFE IS A SUBSTANCE IN A CONTAINER; LIFE IS BEING PRESENT HERE; LIFE IS BONDAGE; LIFE IS A BURDEN; HUMAN LIFE IS THE LIFE-CYCLE OF A PLANT.

The metaphor that is going to be especially useful and important for us in relation to HAPPINESS is the JOURNEY metaphor, LIFE IS A JOURNEY metaphor. So let's spell out the major mappings of the JOURNEY metaphor. In the LIFE IS A JOURNEY metaphor, we find the following correspondences. The traveler of course corresponds to the person leading a life. The journey corresponds to living a life. The destination corresponds to the purpose or goal of life. The stages of the journey correspond to stages in life. The distance covered along the journey corresponds to the progress made in life. Path of the journey corresponds to ways of living. Obstacles along the way correspond to difficulties in life. As you very well know, a lot of this has to do with the Events Structure Metaphor, and so that's a well-known story.

Given this very brief characterization of major life metaphors and the LIFE IS A JOURNEY metaphor and its mappings, let's take a look at, perhaps, the best known application or the best known use of the concept of HAPPINESS which can be found in the *American Declaration of Independence*, the *Declaration of Independence*, 1776. So let's read the first two passages of the *Declaration of Independence*. As the historical background, although this is well-known, North America was colonized by the British and there were the

13 colonies and the colonies by the 1770s wanted to become independent from Britain. This *Declaration of Independence* refers to the efforts of the colonies to become independent from Britain. So this is what it says:

> When in the Course of human events it becomes necessary for one people to dissolve the political bands which have connected them with another and to assume among the powers of the earth, the separate and equal station to which the Laws of Nature and of Nature's God entitle them, a decent respect to the opinions of mankind requires that they should declare the causes which impel them to the separation.

This is the important part for us.

We hold these truths to be self-evident, that all men are created equal, that they are endowed by their Creator with certain unalienable Rights, and this is the crucial part, "that among these are Life, Liberty and the pursuit of Happiness". We will concentrate on "pursuit of happiness".

> That to secure these rights, Governments are instituted among Men, deriving their just powers from the consent of the governed,—That whenever any Form of Government becomes destructive of these ends, it is the Right of the People to alter or to abolish it, and to institute new Government, laying its foundation on such principles and organizing its powers in such form, as to them shall seem most likely to effect their Safety and Happiness.

The important part for us is the clause "that among these are Life, Liberty and the pursuit of Happiness". Let's concentrate on this phrase "pursuit of happiness" and how we can possibly interpret this in the context of the *Declaration of Independence*. Well first of all, notice that the phrase "pursuit of happiness" obviously is derived from the word "pursue", the verb "pursue". When you pursue something, you pursue an object. You can pursue an animal, but let's just say it is an object. Now, happiness, however, is a state. Notice that we immediately get a very high level what is called "ontological metaphor" which is STATES ARE OBJECTS. Happiness is a state. It is conceptualized as a moving object that we pursue. So what we get is STATES ARE OBJECTS, more specifically, HAPPINESS IS AN OBJECT. This is an ontological metaphor.

There is some inherent desire if you pursue something. So the phrase "pursuit of happiness" goes together with the idea that you pursue the thing because you want to get it. So we can say that happiness, more specifically, is not simply an object, but HAPPINESS IS A DESIRED OBJECT. In this particular phrase, the "pursuit of happiness", there is this animal-like object that is trying to move away from you and you are trying to catch it. You are trying to get closer and closer to it and eventually get to it and catch it.

However, if we just say that HAPPINESS IS A DESIRED OBJECT, then this metaphor at this particular level comes in two versions. One is where you have the object as an animal that is trying to move away from you and you desire it and that is why you pursue it. But it also comes in another version where the object is hidden and you are trying to find it and you are trying to move close to it and eventually get it.

These are two versions of the same higher-level metaphor which is HAPPINESS IS A DESIRED OBJECT. It comes in two versions, so version one is that we can call more specifically the MOVING DESIRED OBJECT. Given the MOVING DESIRED OBJECT metaphor, we find the following mappings and the following correspondences. The desired object is happiness. The movement of the object away from you is the difficulty of obtaining the object. The pursuer of the object is the person trying to obtain the happiness. The pursuit itself corresponds to trying to obtain or attain happiness. The desire to catch the object corresponds to the desire for happiness, and catching the object corresponds to obtaining happiness.

We find a slightly different set of mappings for the HIDDEN DESIRED OBJECT version of the DESIRED OBJECT metaphor. In that version we find the following mappings: The desired object corresponds to happiness. The "hidden-ness" of the object from us corresponds to the difficulty of obtaining the object. The seeker of the object corresponds to the person trying to obtain happiness. The search, you are trying to find it, corresponds to trying to obtain happiness. The desire to find the object corresponds to the desire, and eventually finding the object corresponds to obtaining happiness. So what we see here, however, is that in the *Declaration of Independence* it is not the second version of the metaphor but the first version of the metaphor that we find. It is the pursuit of happiness in which both the pursuer and the pursuant are moving. The pursuer is trying to get closer and closer to it.

The HAPPINESS IS A DESIRED OBJECT metaphor seems to overlap with the metaphor that I mentioned previously, LIFE IS A JOURNEY metaphor, more specifically A PURPOSEFUL LIFE IS A JOURNEY metaphor. Notice what happens in the A PURPOSEFUL LIFE IS A JOURNEY metaphor. In that metaphor, what we get is that there we have some destinations in the source domain corresponding to some purposes and we want to get to the destinations in the source domain and we want to achieve our purposes in life. When we do get to our destination in the source domain, what corresponds to that in the target domain is that we actually obtain the thing or we do not obtain it. Now, this clearly overlaps with the HAPPINESS IS A DESIRED OBJECT metaphor because when you find the object or when you pursue the object, and you actually catch it, you achieve your purpose and the purpose happens to be "happiness". So in both cases there is a goal that you achieve successfully. However the particular goal that you achieve in life is that happiness as a goal. There is a close connection between the LIFE IS A JOURNEY metaphor and HAPPINESS IS A DESIRED OBJECT.

There is a second metaphor that is crucially important to understand the phrase in the *Declaration of Independence* which has to do with the notion of FREEDOM. FREEDOM TO ACT IS FREEDOM TO MOVE. Notice that this comes from the Event Structure Metaphor where the more general level version of this is ACTION IS MOTION. What does this have to do with "pursuit of happiness" in the Declaration of Independence? Well, you can only achieve your happiness, you can only catch the pursued object if you are not obstructed in your motion toward it. If you are obstructed in your motion toward the object, it is very difficult to catch it. I suggest that in order to achieve your happiness, you must be unobstructed metaphorically in your movement towards it. What we find here is something remarkable.

Notice that the *Declaration of Independence* says "among these are Life, Liberty and the pursuit of Happiness". There are two ways of thinking about this set of concepts: life, liberty, and the pursuit of happiness. You can say that these are simply three independent rights. The *Declaration of Independence* happens to name these three independent right concepts. This is not the way I think this was intended. I think the way it was intended by the authors of the *Declaration of independence* was that these are connected right concepts—this is what my metaphor analysis seems to indicate. HAPPINESS IS A DESIRED OBJECT is tightly connected with the LIFE IS A JOURNEY metaphor, and this is based on or functions against the background of the FREEDOM TO ACT IS FREEDOM TO MOVE conceptual metaphor. In other words, the three metaphors seem to be correlated with the three right concepts here: life, liberty, and the pursuit of happiness. "Life" comes from "LIFE IS A JOURNEY", "Liberty" comes from "FREEDOM TO ACT IS FREEDOM TO MOVE", and "the pursuit of happiness" is related to "HAPPINESS IS A DESIRED OBJECT".

It is a better reading of the *Declaration of Independence* to see these three right concepts not as an independent sequence of concepts but as a meaningful sequence of concepts. So given this interpretation of the phrase "the pursuit of happiness" in the *Declaration of Independence*, I think it makes sense to suggest the following model for HAPPINESS in the *Declaration of Independence*. We have certain goals in life. Happiness is, this is in your handout. Happiness is one of people's main life goals. It is a desired state. It is an inalienable right of all people. And then we have the actions or characteristics of actions in accordance with the goals. It is the responsibility of government to make sure that people can obtain it. People devote their lives to trying to obtain it. It is difficult to obtain. It requires effort to obtain it. It takes a long time to obtain it. Once people have obtained it, it lasts a long time. The desired result is that you achieve your goal in life, which is, of course, happiness.

According to my reading of the *Declaration of Independence,* it suggests that our major life goal is happiness. Furthermore, it is the responsibility of the government to make sure that people can obtain it. So governments according to the *Declaration of Independence* are set up in order to make it possible for people to pursue happiness as a major life goal and to achieve it.

So what conclusions can we draw from all this? Well, one conclusion is that as in the case of many other concepts, especially abstract concepts and contested concepts, we find at least two prototypical cognitive models for happiness and the two models of happiness can be given as "happiness is an immediate response" and "happiness is a value". "Happiness is an immediate response" is characterized by a set of distinctive metonymies indicating physiologically expressive behavioral reactions as well as some inherent concepts. "Happiness is a value" can be given as set of distinctive metaphors, but notice that it is not characterized by any kind of metonymies. It is not characterized by any behavioral, expressive or physiological responses. As a matter of fact, the notion of HAPPINESS in the Declaration seems to do with "happiness is a value" model much more than the "happiness is an immediate response" model.

And finally, what we find in the *Declaration of Independence* is that the *Declaration of Independence* doesn't fully spell out the details of what happiness is. It simply assumes that it is a major life goal and tells us what governments should do in order to allow people to achieve that major life goal.

LECTURE 6

Metonymy: A New Look

First I am going over some well-known examples as a kind of warm-up exercise. These examples will be familiar because they are at least thirty years old. They come from Lakoff and Johnson's *Metaphors We Live By*. Then, on the basis of those examples, I'll try to offer a definition of metonymy that I personally now regard as an old definition, and it comes essentially from a paper that I did with Günter Radden in 1998. So that's the kind of definition that I would like to improve on.

Some well-known examples are "I'm reading *Shakespeare*"; "America doesn't want another *Pearl Harbor*"; "*Washington* is negotiating with *Moscow*"; "*Nixon* bombed Hanoi"; "We need a better *glove* at third base". We need a better glove at third base. If these examples sound familiar, it is because these are examples taken from *Metaphors We Live By*.

Now if we go over these examples, well, we can see that the literal meaning of the examples would be entirely different from the intended metonymic ones. The literal meaning would be something like "Shakespeare was a literary genius" or something like that; "We traveled to Pearl Harbor last year"; "Washington is the capital of the United States"; "Nixon is a former American president", "The glove is too tight for me".

All of these examples that I just gave you are examples of specific cases of what we call "conceptual metonymies". On the analogy of conceptual metaphor, we can also talk about conceptual metonymy.

Let's take a look at some conceptual metonymies and see what other examples we can list underneath them. THE PRODUCER FOR THE PRODUCT, that is the author for the work, more specifically, "I'm reading *Shakespeare*"; "She loves *Picasso*"; "Does he own any *Hemingway*?" THE PLACE FOR THE EVENT: "America doesn't want another *Pearl Harbor*"; "Let's not let *El Salvador* become another *Vietnam*"; "*Watergate* changed our politics". THE PLACE FOR THE

All original audio-recordings and other supplementary material, such as any hand-outs and powerpoint presentations for the lecture series, have been made available online and are referenced via unique DOI numbers on the website www.figshare.com. They may be accessed via a QR code for the print version of this book. In the e-book, both the QR code and dynamic links are available, and can be accessed by a mouse-click.

© ZOLTÁN KÖVECSES. REPRODUCED WITH KIND PERMISSION FROM THE AUTHOR BY KONINKLIJKE BRILL NV, LEIDEN, 2020 | DOI:10.1163/9789004364905_007

INSTITUTION: "*Washington* is negotiating with *Moscow*"; "The *White House* isn't saying anything"; "*Wall Street* is in a panic"; "*Hollywood* is putting out terrible movies". THE CONTROLLER FOR THE CONTROLLED: "*Nixon* bombed Hanoi"; "*Ozawa* gave a terrible concert last night". AN OBJECT USED FOR THE USER: "We need a better *glove* at third base"; "The *sax* has the flu today". These are the original formulations of these metonymies in that early work in 1980.

In addition to such conceptual metonymies, a large number of others have been discovered by all kinds of scholars in the field. So we have obviously PART FOR A WHOLE: "We need some good *heads* on the project." WHOLE FOR THE PART: "*America* is a powerful county" where obviously by *America* what you mean is the United States is a powerful country. INSTRUMENT FOR ACTION: "She *shampooed* her hair." EFFECT FOR CAUSE: "It's a *slow* road." PLACE FOR ACTION: actually we have seen this—"America doesn't want another *Pearl Harbor*". DESTINATION FOR MOTION: "He *porched* the newspaper". PLACE FOR PRODUCT: "Give me my *java* or *mocha*." I don't know coffee, it's about coffee. TIME FOR AN OBJECT: "The *8:40* just arrived." This is about the train that is supposed to arrive at 8:40.

Now what we can say about these examples is that in all of them, we have a vehicle entity and we also have what we can call a target entity. Notice that this is comparable to the source domain/target domain distinction in metaphor theory. At the same time, it is different, it is mostly different because the vehicle entity and the target entity in metonymy are supposed to be within the same domain. Now the traditional definition of metonymy, I mean the really traditional definition of metonymy is that it is a relationship of proximity or a relationship of contiguity. When there are two entities close to each other and one is used to refer to the other, that's when you get metonymy. This was the classical way of approaching metonymy.

In Cognitive Linguistics, one of the first improved versions of metonymy comes from the article that I mentioned before. In that article, and in my book, *Metaphor: A Practical Introduction*, I provided the following, that new definition of metonymy that is supposed to be more compatible with certain cognitive linguistic ideas. In that definition, metonymy is a cognitive process in which one conceptual entity, the vehicle, provides mental access to another conceptual entity, the target, within the same domain or idealized cognitive model. So this is more in line with cognitive linguistic notions such as metonymy being a mental process, a cognitive operation, or a conceptual operation.

This is far from being a perfect definition. I want to give you one reason why it is not, and that leads us to a major problem with it, which is that in many cases on the basis of this definition. It will be very difficult to say whether we have metaphor or metonymy. In order to show some difficult cases where this discrepancy can happen, let's look at some examples. "He is in low spirits", which means someone is sad. "She is feeling up", which means someone is happy. "He is a hothead", which means someone is angry.

Now the question is: Are these metaphoric or metonymic expressions? The definition said that we have metonymy where one entity—the vehicle entity—is used to provide mental access to the target entity within the same frame; what Lakoff would call the idealized cognitive model. However, this is a big issue when the vehicle entity and the target entity are within the same frame, and when is the case that we can legitimately say that they are outside or one of them is outside that frame.

Now if we look at these examples and take the first one—"he is in low spirits", this is what everybody has been saying since Lakoff and Johnson, that SAD IS DOWN is one of the prime examples of conceptual metaphor; HAPPY IS UP, one of the prime examples of another conceptual metaphor; ANGER IS HEAT—these are what I call prime examples of conceptual metaphors. I would say that there is a problem, because we can interpret all of these cases as not simply metaphoric, but also as metonymic. I want to take you through a possible interpretation where it would make, to my mind at least, perfect sense to say that these are metonymic rather than metaphoric expressions.

One of what I called the behavioral responses associated with sadness is drooping posture, the mouth being turned off. These are some of the behavioral responses that we produce when we are intensely sad. In all these cases, there is some kind of downward bodily orientation. The same would go for happiness, where we can say associated moods have an upward bodily orientation. Now if sadness goes together with a downward bodily orientation like mouth being turned off and drooping body posture, then we can say in a perfectly legitimate sense that the downward bodily orientation is inside the sadness frame—we are talking about sadness. This is obviously in the domain of sadness. Now if that is the case, there is no way that I want to call this expression "he is in low spirits" a metaphoric expression. For example, "she is feeling up", is a metaphoric expression, and "he is a hothead" is a metaphoric one. I can equally well say that, these are metonymies. These are metonymies because what they describe is a particular bodily orientation in this case, and downward bodily orientation is inside the sadness frame. So there is no problem with taking this particular expression as a metonymic one. However these are major examples of metaphor. We don't want to not believe the founding fathers, but I think we can make a good case here to not believe them.

How can we build a metaphoric interpretation for the same thing? We can say that downward bodily orientation is at a very specific level of generalization.

METONYMY: A NEW LOOK   69

At a higher level of generalization, we would have DOWN, or DOWNWARD, or something like that. Notice that what I left out is some of the features of DOWNWARD BODILY orientation. This is exactly the concept of DOWN that I assume Lakoff and Johnson first had in mind when they set up the SAD IS DOWN and the HAPPY IS UP metaphors.

So what seems to be going on to my mind is that downward bodily orientation as a very specific level response is generalized into DOWN or DOWNWARD as a concept. This is divorced and distinct from the actual response or responses that we see in sadness or happiness. This would be way outside the sadness frame if you think about it this way. So you generalize it into the concept of DOWN, you go outside the sadness frame and you are, let's say, in the SPACE frame.

So if you think of all this in terms of hierarchical structures in the conceptual system, then you can say that sadness is somewhere in the emotion system, but the concept of DOWN and the concept of UP and the concept of HEAT are in entirely different vertical hierarchies of the conceptual system. In the case of heat, you would have a temperature hierarchy. Obviously because we are talking about entirely different vertical taxonomies or hierarchies here, we could say that the source domain and the target domain are entirely different from each other. They are distinct from each other in conceptual space. As a result, we can legitimately call them metaphors. However, if you think of downward bodily orientation in more specific terms, then it is equally legitimate to call them metonymies. I think this makes a lot of sense to think about it this way.

Let's take another example, INTIMACY IS CLOSENESS, another well-known conceptual metaphor. However, I want to suggest that we can also conceptualize it differently and we can conceptualize it as a metonymy. When we do that, what we get is something like PHYSICAL CLOSENESS BETWEEN TWO PEOPLE FOR INTIMACY and that is intended to indicate a metonymic, not a metaphoric relationship. But we can make the same kind of argument here that we made in the previous case of sadness. We can say that when we talk about intimacy, and we think of for example children who are usually in very intimate relation let's say with their mothers and they are very close to each other most of the time, especially the first few years of life. We can say that this is a physical closeness between two people, and this is also a very specific level of generalization, and it is inside what we would call the intimacy frame. Because this is inside the intimacy frame, and it is a reflection of how people are intimate, we can call it a metonymy.

However, the same argument applies here that applied before in the case of sadness. We can say that the physical intimacy between two people can be generalized into something higher level in another part of the conceptual system, which would be CLOSENESS.

Notice that we are talking about closeness here, not necessarily between two people, but between any two objects. This is a more abstract understanding or conceptualization of physical closeness between two people. This would be a very general kind of relationship between any two objects. If you do that, that concept of CLOSENESS would not be inside the domain or inside the frame of INTIMACY. It would be in an entirely different part of the conceptual system.

It would be again somewhere in the space HIERARCHY, where we talk about particular relationships—spatial relationships between objects, such that they can be close, they can be distant, and so on so forth. When that is the case, intimacy is conceptualized in terms of an entirely different concept from another part of the conceptual system. It would be appropriate to call this a metaphor. This is indeed what has been going on in the cognitive literature. I would like to suggest that we can also think of it as a metonymy.

Now as a matter of fact, Lakoff and Johnson, especially inspired by the work of Grady, in 1999's *Philosophy of the Flesh* say that metaphor is not based on any kind of similarity. Certain types of metaphor, mainly primary metaphors are not based on any kind of similarity. So what my argument would imply is that everything that they call primary metaphor is in reality metonymy. I'm inclined to accept that. If they are in the same domain, or if they can be shown to be in the same domain, and I think in the case of intimacy and physical closeness between two people, you can argue that it is the case. This is primarily a metonymy, not a metaphor. Because the same argument would go for all the cases that Grady calls primary metaphor, I would suggest that all primary metaphors are, at least initially, can be regarded as metonymies.

Interestingly, this kind of duality in the way we look at the relationship between the source entity and the target entity has been noticed before. Eve Sweetser noticed it, for example. In her 1990 book, for example, Sweetser characterizes the relationship between visual monitoring and control in the following way. "The basis for this metaphor is probably the fact that guarding or keeping control often involves visual monitoring of the controlled entity; and the limited domain of physical vision is further analogous to the domain of personal influence of control."

In other words, what she is saying, is that the relationship between visual monitoring and control which is called the CONTROL IS SEEING, CONTROL IS VISION conceptual metaphor can essentially be thought about in two ways. It can be thought about as a metaphor where you would have control and seeing coming from completely different parts of the conceptual system, as opposed to VISUAL MONITORING FOR GUARDING, which are much more specific level instances of vision and control, while however, they are within the same domain. When we guard something, we track where the object goes, and as a part of guarding, we perform this kind of visual activity. So we have to do with the same domain.

The same argument would go for the well-known metaphor, KNOWING OR KNOWLEDGE IS SEEING. In the case of metonymy, or in the case of some examples we can interpret at a very specific level—certain connected entities within the same domain are being linked as metonymies because the two entities, like the ones we have seen so far, are or can be said to be in the same domain.

However, this is happening at a fairly specific level. In the case of metaphor, you generalize these specific level instances to higher levels, and when you do that, in the case of control and in the case of vision, let's say, you will end up with a concept, a very abstract concept like "control" and a much less abstract concept like "vision", which are obviously in different parts of the conceptual system. These are cases that we can call metaphor. It seems to me that the original Lakoff and Johnson idea misses the more specific interpretation of particular frames, where we can legitimately see the source entity and the target entity as belonging together in the same frame.

This is the problem for my old definition, but at the same time, I think it takes us further and it at least gives us a chance to think more about the nature of the distinction between metaphor and metonymy. This would be my way of characterizing one of the differences between metaphor and metonymy.

Ok, now let me very briefly turn to what is called the neural theory of metaphor and metonymy today. This was more or less initiated by George Lakoff and Jerome Feldman in Berkeley. I will take up this issue only because there is going to be some similarity between the new view of metonymy and this neural theory of metaphor and metonymy that George Lakoff has been proposing recently. I especially have in mind his article in the *Cambridge Handbook of Metaphor* published in 2008.

If we look at the history of the study of metaphor and metonymy, what we find is that originally metaphor and metonymy were issues dealt with in language. This is something that Lakoff and Johnson keep pointing out that they want to break away from that tradition. And then they proposed that in addition to being an issue in language, metaphor and metonymy are also major issues in conceptual structure. Metaphor and metonymy are conceptual in nature, not only linguistic. This extension of the ontology of metaphor and metonymy was taken further into the human body. What that means is that when you look for motivation for metaphors especially, what we find is that there are certain bodily experiences that seem to provide the motivation for metaphors and also for metonymies as we saw in the case of emotions.

So we have these three very different realms where we can detect metaphor and metonymy. I don't know whether this is the final extension, but this extension takes us into the neural system. It takes us to the brain. The discussion now is at the level of the brain, and we are trying to connect what we know about metaphor and metonymy linguistically, conceptually and experientially with what we know or what we are trying to find out about metaphor and metonymy in the brain. Of course there is a fifth level. Actually the fifth level came earlier than the fourth level, and that's the level of course, the context. That's where I try to work. For example, in *Metaphor in Culture*, I try to work out the implications of the influence of culture on metaphorical conceptualization. So these are more or less the five important, ontological levels where we have to deal with the issue of metaphor and metonymy.

Now Lakoff and Johnson say that there are neurons in the brain, well of course they are not neural scientists, and this is more or less a computational model of metaphor and metonymy that they are proposing. We will have to see whether this will be actually found experimentally by real neural scientists who are doing actual research on the brain.

So there are neural bindings between neurons or groups of neurons. Two or more conceptual entities are taken to be a single entity in the neural binding. For example, the way we understand a blue square, comes from the neural binding of the domain of color and the domain of space.

Now what is immediately important for us in the study of metonymy and metaphor is the following. Lakoff suggests that there are different types of neural circuits—what he calls the linking circuits are what is responsible for metonymy. A linking circuit is simply based on the definition that I gave you previously—a vehicle entity provides mental access to another entity, the target. What Lakoff is saying here is basically a neural scientific version of that idea. There are two-way linking circuits. These are responsible for words and grammatical constructions where you have a form and meaning pairing and two-way linking circuits, because you can go from the form to the meaning and from the meaning to the form. Finally, we have what he calls mapping circuits. This is what's responsible for metaphor.

Now let me try to go on to what I take to be a new definition, an improved definition, of the one that I gave you at the beginning. So it seems to me that in general in the conceptual system, we can distinguish between three types of connections. One is what I call a through-connection. This is simply a generalization of the part of the definition that I mentioned before, that the source entity provides mental access to the target entity. And I call this a through-connection.

So if you imagine the conceptual system, however the conceptual system is structured, there are conceptual entities in that structure and when it is the case that one entity in that structure is used to provide access to another entity in the structure, then you have a through-connection. And through-connections I assume are metonymies. In the case of metaphor, however, I would say that there are as-if-connections. That is, you take a conceptual entity as if it was or as if it were another conceptual entity. That's what happens in a metaphor. We also have is-connections that we often find in between mental spaces. This is the kind of work that Fauconnier works on. We use is-connections to make identifications between conceptual entities in different mental spaces. An entity in one mental space is identified with another entity in another mental space. And that's what I call an is-connection.

Now what I call through-connections in my view can be of two kinds. They can be, metaphorically speaking, outward-looking or inward-looking. Outward-looking mappings activate an entity that is outside the primary domain. I am using primary domain in Langacker's sense, or our central knowledge.

So when, for example, you have "I bought another *Hemingway*". It points to a secondary domain for Hemingway, which is his books. So this would be an outside-looking kind of mapping. Inward-looking mappings activate something inside the primary domain. "This book is large." The word *book* provides a difficult case of course what counts as a primary domain and what counts as a secondary domain.

Langacker says that "physical object" is certainly a primary domain for a book, because books are physical objects. It's another question whether the semantic content of a book would also count as a primary domain or would be a secondary domain.

Now because books are characterized by such domains as physical objects, shape, size, color, and so on, and when we say the book is large, obviously this has to do with book as a physical object, we would say this is an inward-looking mapping. I would say that this is an inward-looking mapping, as opposed to the previous example, when you have something like "I bought another Hemingway".

Now, as I said, it is sometimes difficult to say what is primary and what is secondary, maybe we have a gradient of primariness and you know this complicates issues a little bit. So we can ask whether "this book is complicated" is an inward or an outward looking mapping. The answer depends on how you decide on, or what you decide on the issue of whether the content of a book, because "complicated" refers to the content of the book, not the book as a physical object, how you answer that question. Is it a primary domain or a secondary domain? Now outward-looking mappings either refer to an entity or highlight an aspect of a concept. An outward-looking mapping referring to an entity would be, for example, "I bought another Hemingway", as I mentioned previously. However, an outward-looking mapping can also highlight an aspect of a concept as in "This book is complicated", if you decide that this is a secondary domain. Inward-looking metonymic mappings only highlight an aspect of a concept or an entity. So when you say "This book is large", to my mind at least, this is an inward-looking mapping that highlights an aspect of the entity BOOK.

Now well of course we are running into a major problem with all this, and the major problem that is obviously here, I am talking about what is known as "active zone" as proposed by Langacker. Now the question is, are all cases of active zone phenomena metonymies or not? What can we do about this particular issue? Some people suggest that we can delimit active zone phenomena and suggest that not all active zone cases are metonymies, if we assume that one of the criteria features of metonymy is a shift in meaning.

If you take, for example, "I admire Hemingway", and what you mean is that you have Hemingway as an author in mind with his authorial qualities, when you say "I admire Hemingway", and you mean his authorial qualities, this would not be a metonymy. Why? Because the authorial qualities of an author are not conventionalized new senses of the author.

So, and the argument would be that because you don't have a shift in meaning, you have no metonymy in such cases as "I admire Hemingway". So what can we do now? When you say "I bought another Hemingway", we have to do with a metonymy. Why? Because there is a conventionalized new sense for Hemingway, with all authors as a matter of fact, namely, that an author is not simply an author, you can in a conventionalized way make reference to the author's products or the author's books. And because there is a recognized conventionalized shift in, you would have metonymy here.

Now I do not really agree with this kind of argument, however. I would imagine that even if we don't have conventionalized shift, what we have is a momentary act of highlighting a particular aspect of an entity. I think this is what is happening in all active zone cases. So I am taking a very radical view and I would assume that all active zone cases are instances of metonymy. I do not think that the shifts in a conventionalized sense really invalidate this kind of assumption on my part, because even though there is no shift in conventionalized sense, there is a brief momentary highlighting of an aspect of a particular domain or entity.

Given this way of talking about metonymy, this is my hopefully new and improved version of metonymy. In metonymy, we access entity 2 through entity 1 by means of a "through-connection". Entity 1 and 2 are concepts and—by concepts and also entity, I mean also subdomain, or, in the case of entity 2, aspects of concepts—the two are in the same ICM, or frame. The mapping can be either inward-looking or outward-looking. If it is outward-looking, it can result either in entity 1 referring to entity 2 or entity 1 highlighting an aspect of entity 2. This was "the book is complicated" example. If it is inward-looking, entity 1 highlights an aspect of the same entity. This was "this book is large". So this would be a new definition of metonymy, hopefully an improved one, and on the basis of this, we can obviously discover a large number of different interpretations of what metonymy is or ways of conceptualizing metonymy.

I would suggest this definition also implies a particular prototype for metonymy. And the prototype of metonymy could be given as follows. There is a through-connection between entity 1 and entity 2. Entity 1 and entity 2 are concepts or subdomains within a larger domain. There is a pragmatic function mapping between entity 1 and entity 2. We need this to ensure that the two entities are within the same domain. The mappings between entity 1 and entity 2, the mapping between entity 1 and entity 2 is outward-looking. And entity 1 refers to entity 2.

However, as I said, this is only the characterization of the prototype. An obvious non-prototypical definition would be the one in which entity 1 highlights an aspect of entity 2. But in the prototypical case, I think metonymy is used to refer. This is what Lakoff and Johnson had in mind thirty years ago, but they disregarded all the other potential cases of metonymy.

LECTURE 7

A New View of Metaphorical Creativity I

Good morning, everyone. Let's going to talk about metaphorical creativity, which is a relatively neglected field in the study of metaphor in Cognitive Linguistics. The major question that I'm going to ask is: Where do we recruit novel and unconventional conceptual materials from when we speak and think metaphorically—and why? I made an attempt to come up with some kind of an answer in my *Metaphor in Culture* in 2005 where I distinguished two essential types of metaphorical creativity: "source-related" creativity and "target-related" creativity. "Source-related" creativity can come in two kinds: it can be "source-internal" and "source-external". It was primarily Lakoff and Turner who worked on the issue of "source-internal" creativity where, when they in their *More Than Cool Reason* came up with the idea that given a particular source domain, what often happens, for example, in poetry, is that poets either elaborate, expand, question, or combine what they find in the source domain. So one of the nice examples that Lakoff and Turner discuss in *More Than Cool Reason* is from Hamlet—the great soliloquy by Hamlet where he says "to die, to sleep, no more, perchance to dream ..." and so on and so forth. Notice that this is based on the DEATH IS SLEEP metaphor. However, when Hamlet says "to die, to sleep", what happens is that he elaborates or extends the notion of sleep, with "perchance" to dream he is extending the notion of sleep to dreaming.

This is one way in which Lakoff and Turner try to capture the idea that it is not simply highly conventionalized sets of mappings that characterize particular conceptual metaphors. The "source-external" kind of creativity is a very simple idea. What it simply means is that you have a particular set of source domains for a particular target domain, and then you add newer and newer source domains to capture the target domain.

All original audio-recordings and other supplementary material, such as any hand-outs and powerpoint presentations for the lecture series, have been made available online and are referenced via unique DOI numbers on the website www.figshare.com. They may be accessed via a QR code for the print version of this book. In the e-book, both the QR code and dynamic links are available, and can be accessed by a mouse-click.

© ZOLTÁN KÖVECSES. REPRODUCED WITH KIND PERMISSION FROM THE AUTHOR BY KONINKLIJKE
BRILL NV, LEIDEN, 2020 | DOI:10.1163/9789004364905_008

Now the "target-related" kind of creativity is more interesting, and I also discussed that in the book that I mentioned. This happens when a particular target that is conventionally associated with a source "connects back" to the source taking further knowledge structures from it. One example of this was found at the time of the unification of European in 1990s, Gorbachev, the Russian president, introduced the metaphor of the European house, so European unity is a house. Now given that metaphor there are some obvious and conventional mappings that constitute it.

So for example the structure of the house corresponds to the structure of the political unity of the European Union. However, given the target domain, there are certain issues that emerge. One of the issues that can emerge from the target domain is that we join the European Union but what happens if you want to leave it. This was part of the debate that was going on about the unification of Europe in the 1990s. Given this idea is in the target domain, you can connect back to the source domain and you can try to find a particular element in the source domain that you could use to express that element in the target domain. The particular item that was used was a fire-exit. Houses have fire-exits, and so if you want to leave the European Union, will there be a fire-exit to leave it? So this is however not part of the conventionalized set of mappings in the EUROPEAN UNION IS A BUILDING metaphor, it is derived from the target—you look for some materials in the source and then apply that to the target again.

So these are the two general kinds of creativity that have been discussed so far in the literature and what I would like to do is to go beyond these kinds of metaphorical creativity and introduce a new one that was not really discussed by conceptual metaphor theory scholars. This is what I would call "context-induced creativity". Analogously I will talk about "context-induced metaphors".

I will be talking about five different contexts, what I call immediate contexts, the immediate physical setting, what we know about the major entities participating in the discourse, the immediate cultural context, the immediate social context, and the immediate linguistic context itself.

I propose that a large number of metaphors that we find in everyday discourse can be characterized by thinking of creativity this way. However, I also want to propose that somewhat surprisingly poetic creativity in metaphor also, can also be explained quite often on the basis of what I call "context-induced creativity". As I mentioned, the only explanation for metaphorical creativity in poetry was Lakoff and Turner's explanation in terms of elaboration, extending, questioning and combining metaphors in the source domain. However, I would like to offer this new view of context-induced creativity. This is not to deny that others have not thought about this issue. For example, Fauconnier and Turner do so in their 2002 book, where they discussed the concept of blending or conceptual integration, they proposed that what very often happens in metaphorical creativity in poetry can be explained by what they call blending or conceptual integration. Now my particular approach to metaphorical creativity as you will see will differ considerably from all of these approaches. I hope I will be in a position to convince you that this is a very appropriate and legitimate kind of approach to the issue of metaphorical creativity.

This whole issue of creativity is of course connected with the very general issue of universality and variation in metaphor. When we talk about creativity we are talking about variation. In Cognitive Linguistics, it seems to me that the predominant trend of research has been focusing on universality in metaphorical conceptualization. The theory of primary metaphor only reinforces that focus on universality—there are probably very good reasons for focusing on universality in conceptual metaphor theory.

However, I would like to propose another line of research and that started with my *Metaphor in Culture* book in 2005 where I proposed that we have to take into account context, because it is context that can explain variation and more specifically creativity.

Now I distinguish between two kinds of context—global context and local context. By global context I don't mean universal. By global context I mean the context that is somehow assumed by a particular language community. I will go through some examples in a minute. By local context I mean the immediate contextual factors that apply to a particular conceptualizer in a particular communicative situation. However, I have to make it very clear that the notion of global context and the notion of immediate context form a gradient, and it is not a yes or no kind of distinction. They don't have very clear boundaries. Very often they overlap with each other, as some of the examples will indicate.

Now let me first give you some examples of what I mean by global context. Many languages or many dialects of languages assume a particular physical environment. So up until, let's say, the 17th or 18th century, English was primarily used on the British isles and a certain kind of metaphorical conceptual system emerged that may use that physical environment including the general landscape, the fauna, the flora, the kinds of houses, the people, and so on and so forth. These are all parts of the physical environment. Given this physical environment that was used sometimes conventionally, sometimes very creatively, for example, by Shakespeare, was changed considerably when the English language was transported, so to speak, to the North American continent. On the North American continent, many aspects of the physical environment changed, and with that the metaphors changed.

In several publications I have tried to describe some of the changes that have occurred in that process. If you look at them in other languages, for example, Dutch, the way it was spoken in the 18th century, and then taken to to South Africa, with completely different fauna and flora and geography change, the underlying system of metaphors in Dutch also changed, as Rene Dirven describes very nicely.

Social factors are extremely complex and they have many aspects. What I mean by social factors includes the distinction between women and men. To take an interesting example where women seem to be using metaphors that are consistently different from the metaphors that men use, let me take again the history of the United States. One literary scholar in the United States wrote two very interesting books. The books are not explicitly devoted to these issues. It's primarily a literary kind of approach. But some of the examples that she uses or some of the conclusions that she arrives at provide us with a very nice idea of how social factors such as the distinction between men and women can provide very different metaphorical use of the same thing.

Annette Kolodny is the name of the author, and in her studies she looks at 300 years of literary documents about the United States concerning the early settlers in 17th, 18th, and 19th centuries. She looks at American literature. She looks at personal documents like letters and biography and so on and so forth. She concludes that, on the basis of this huge amount of material, American women conceptualized North America as a garden. As opposed to women, men conceptualized North America as virgin land to be taken. This is a striking difference. After all, both the men and the women live in the same place, but it seems that the overall image that they produce for themselves, given the same subject matter, produce very, very different metaphors.

Let's consider the cultural context. By the cultural context, by the broad, by the global cultural context, I mean some of the major principles that govern the functioning of a particular culture, some of the key ideas that can be found in a culture. A very nice example of this is provided by Chinese culture where, to the best of my knowledge, the concept of *qi* is a crucially important idea and it is not surprising for that reason that the notion of *qi* shows up in all kinds of metaphors, like metaphors for anger. However, in Europe where *qi* does not really exist, there was an entirely different principle, which we call the "four humors" that provided a very different outlook on emotions.

What differential memory simply means is history. I refer to it as differential memory because each and every society has a different kind of history and somehow we can think of history as memory. Now it seems that there can be major differences given a particular global context. We can take for an example that of the United States and Hungary—one of my students did an interesting study on these two countries. She interviewed Americans and Hungarians about their conceptions of life. She was of course interested in the major metaphors that organize their concept of LIFE and their understanding of the meaning of life.

It turned out that Americans, life was conceptualized as a precious object and as a game, whereas for Hungarians, life was conceptualized as struggle, and it was conceptualized as compromise. I think it immediately makes sense to understand this difference. The major reason probably lies in the difference between Hungarian history and American history. Hungary, as you may know, for 1000 years, has been a small country that lies between very powerful Slavik nations like Russia and very powerful Germanic nations like Germany and Austria. They constantly have had to fight for survival. Because of this it makes a lot of sense for Hungarians to think of life as struggle and compromise, whereas an American life is primarily a precious object.

Ok, now the last aspect of what I mean by global context is differential concerns and interests, that is, the major interests that characterize a particular culture as a whole. These are often based on stereotypes, but nevertheless the stereotypes seem to derive different metaphorical conceptions. One example of this could be again the United States and another could be Britain. As several authors, such as Anna Wierzbicka, point out, there's an interesting difference between Americans and the British and that is Americans are a lot more dynamic, a lot more action-oriented, purpose-goal-oriented, in comparison to the British.

Now this is reflected in the way Americans commonly overuse sports metaphors, which pervade any kind of discussion in the United States. It is also seen at other levels of language, which seems to be the reason why Americans, for example, talk about taking a shower and taking a break as opposed to the British who talk about having a shower. To Wierzbicka, these differences are indications of the very different concerns and interests of these two nations.

Now let me turn to the local context, that is, the immediate contexts and how they seem to have influence on metaphorical conceptualization. Many of the cases that I will discuss produce what we can take to be novel metaphors. However, in some of the other cases, the metaphors that are produced simply can be seen simply as motivating the choice or the selection of a particular metaphor rather than another out of equally valid possibilities.

Let me begin with the effect of the immediate physical setting on metaphor use. In 2007 an American journalist went to New Orleans to do an interview with the famous American rock musician Fats Domino, you may have heard this name. He did the interview with him because of course everyone in America and throughout the world was curious about what happened to New Orleans after the 2005 hurricane which devastated New Orleans, and Fats Domino lives in New Orleans. Now this is what the journalist expressed in his article. "The 2005 hurricane capsized Domino's life, though he's loath to confess any inconvenience or misery outside of missing his social circle ..." The particular metaphor that interests me here is "capsize", which is of course an example you can say of the LIFE IS A JOURNEY metaphor. It is more specifically the LIFE IS A SEA JOURNEY metaphor.

But there are many equally good options that could have been used here, but the journalist decided to use this one. I would like to suggest that this is because even at the time of the interview, there were still overturned boats and ships and an unbelievable amount of devastation still visible in New Orleans two years after the event. So in that context, this seems to be a perfectly fitting kind of metaphor rather than something else. If the journalist wanted to stick to this metaphor, he could have used "his life ran aground", let's say. But "capsize", the way boats overturn seems to be a much more appropriate kind of metaphor.

I want to extend the same argument to poetry, and explain some uses of poetry in the same way—that is, in terms of the global and local context or immediate context. To see this, I'm going to quickly recite to you two stanzas from a well-known poem by Matthew Arnold called *Dover Beach*.

Before I do that let me just say that in poetry poets can do essentially two things with the immediate physical context. What they can do is that they can describe it more or less literally, or they may use the context as a means of talking about something else. Of course that is what we are interested in because when I say as a means of talking about something else that is when they speak metaphorically and make use of the context.

So let's see this poem *Dover Beach* by Matthew Arnold, the first stanza and the last one.

> The sea is calm to-night.
> The tide is full, the moon lies fair
> Upon the straits,—on the French coast, the light
> Gleams and is gone; the cliffs of England stand,
> Glimmering and vast, out in the tranquil bay.
> Come to the window, sweet is the night-air!

Ok, so this is the first stanza, which is a more or less faithful literal transcription or description of the physical context. He describes what he can see, what he can see on the beach, what he can see on the other side off the channel, the

French coast, and the lights and the evening air is sweet, and all these things. This is a more or less literary description of what is going on and he looks at all these from inside a little cottage where he is standing someday with his wife, this is why he says "come to the window, sweet is the night-air". Now in contrast to this, let's take a look at the last stanza where we find the following:

> The sea of Faith
> Was once, too, at the full, and round earth's shore
> Lay like the folds of a bright girdle furled.
> But now I only hear
> Its melancholy, long, withdrawing roar,
> Retreating, to the breath
> Of the night-wind, down the vast edges drear
> And naked shingles of the world.

Obviously, this is much more metaphorical. In the last stanza there are three crucially important metaphors that provide us with the possible interpretation of the poem that is based on the immediate physical context. Well, obviously the main metaphor is "the sea of faith" that begins the stanza. With "the sea of faith", we can capture that in terms of conceptual metaphor theory as CHRISTIAN FAITH, CHRISTIAN FAITH IS THE SEA and THE PEOPLE ARE THE LAND. This is one set of connected metaphors here. There are two other important metaphors—HEALTHY IS WHOLENESS and PERFECTION IS ROUNDNESS, HEALTHY IS WHOLENESS and PERFECTION IS ROUNDNESS. Notice what is going on as he looks out of the window and sees the ebb and flow of the sea, the sea moves way out and you can see, the sea shore, the sea bank, and it is completely exposed to any dangers you can say metaphorically. So we can ask what is the danger. Well, what he is talking about here, literary historians say, is that we are in the 19th century, that's when the poem was written. The dominance of Christianity began to almost disappear in England at the time. He finds this very unfortunate because now with the disappearance of Christianity the world is becoming a much less healthy and a much less perfect place. This is why we have the other two metaphors where HEALTHY IS WHOLENESS. Notice that there was a time in human history when the metaphorical sea completely surrounded and wrapped people—the land. Now the sea is retreating and it is exposing people to all kinds of dangers. The other, PERFECTION IS ROUNDNESS, the sea was all around, it protected people, that is, Christian faith protected people from all kinds of dangers that are now lurking around them.

So my argument would be that Matthew Arnold, as he was looking out of the window of his cottage, conceptualizes a metaphorical idea inspired by what he actually sees in the physical environment at that moment. I am not suggesting of course that he wrote the poem immediately on spot. I'm suggesting instead that this is the immediate physical experience that he must have carried home, at least at the time he wrote the poem.

So in poetry I am not saying that the immediate context immediately affects metaphorical conceptualization, but that it affects metaphorical conceptualization in a similar way to what we saw in the case of the example of the "capsize" example that affects the Domino article.

Now the next type of example that I would like to look at is the effect of knowledge about major entities in the discourse on metaphor use. By the major entities, what I simply mean is the topic, the conceptualizer, and the other conceptualizer—the addressee or the hearer. Now to give you a sense of how the topic can affect and influence a particular metaphorical conceptualization, let me give you a deliberately humorous example that is very often used and is a very common strategy in newspaper headlines. Possibly if I give you the following headline, you would not be able to make sense of it, but then I will read what this newspaper article says about it. "Foot heads arms body", all body parts, this is a headline in a newspaper. How did it come about? In the *London Times* there is a particular column for letters to the editor, and someone writes a letter to the editor:

> Sir, The letters about odd headlines ... reminded me of an all-time favourite. In the early 1980s Michael Foot became the leader of the Labour Party. He was also a co-founder of Committee for Nuclear Disarmament and pushed for nuclear disarmament. Mr. Foot travelled to Brussels to chair a lobby group in the European Parliament to construct a plan to get rid of the bomb as part of the European election policy. From this came the headline "Foot heads arms body".

So this is my point, you have one of the major elements in the discourse, one of the major elements of course is this person called Foot, Mr. Foot. Given that you built a whole series of metaphors and metonymies on this basis of "Foot heads arms body", it makes perfect sense if you know the context.

This is a very conscious kind of example of course. The next example that I want to discuss is much less conscious, as you will see. We can suggest that it is entirely unconscious. It comes from an American magazine and this is how it goes:

> In the beginning, I didn't make the connection between the subject matter and my own sero-positivity. I was asked to be part of the Day Without Art exhibition a few years ago and didn't think I was worthy—other artists' work was much more HIV-specific.... But my mentor said, "Don't you see the connection? You're documenting something that was never intended to live this long. You never intended to live this long."

This passage is about an American photographer who lives in New York, and he has AIDS. He has a mentor. He goes to the mentor and the mentor tells him this. The photographer photographs mural advertisements on old New York City buildings. Let's say 100 years ago, 150 years ago, there were big advertisements painted on the walls of some of the old houses in New York. He was taking photographs of those. He is a photographic artist. And then his mentor says "Don't you see the connection? You're documenting something that was never intended to live this long. You never intended to live this long." Now this is an amazing example because unconsciously the photographer is doing something that is based on a metaphor. We can say that the metaphor is something like this: SURVIVING AIDS DESPITE PREDICTIONS TO THE CONTRARY IS FOR THE OLD MURAL ADVERTISEMENTS TO SURVIVE THEIR EXPECTED "LIFE SPAN".

So in the same way as those New York City buildings with the old advertisements were not intended to last 100 or 150 years. He was not intended to live this long after he was diagnosed with AIDS. He is setting up an unconscious metaphor to do this. This is what I mean when I say that knowledge about the conceptualizer can help us or can trigger or I would even say prompt or prime the selection of particular metaphor.

Let's see an example about the topic and the addressee again. I gave you an example of topic but let me give you another one because it also provides us with an example for how knowledge about the addressee might have an influence on the creation of metaphors. This is a newspaper article about David Beckham, the well-known English football player. The newspaper article is about why the new Italian coach of the English football team doesn't want to play him at a particular game although that would be the 100th time he plays for the English national team. This is a excerpt from that article: "Beckham is 32. He has not played top-class football since November. Los Angeles Galaxy are sardines, not sharks, in the ocean of footy."

Those of you who follow football should know that for a while Beckham played for the Los Angeles Galaxy to make money. Capello doesn't want to play him on the national team because he feels that he is out of shape. The article says "He has not played top-class football since November. Los Angeles

Galaxy are sardines not sharks in the ocean of footy", which is an interesting metaphor.

The question is how does the journalist arrive at this particular metaphor? What we can say here is that we have a certain amount of knowledge about Beckham. We know that he is a football player. And we know that he plays for the Los Angeles Galaxy. We know that Los Angeles is a big city in California on the ocean, on the Pacific Ocean, and we know that the associated frame with Los Angeles is that it is on the Pacific Ocean and that the Pacific Ocean has all kinds of fish including these fish. So given what we know about the topic, in this case Beckham, helps us understand in the same way as it helped create for the author of the article this particular metaphor.

Now in the same article the letter begins: "Dear *Signor* Capello, Beckham is a good footballer and a nice man"—and now you should forgive my Italian—"*e una bella figura*", which means "and a nice figure"—something like that. This shows I think that even the addressee, the person to whom we're talking can have a subtle influence on the way we conceptualize something in context. This is I'm told a very conventional Italian metaphor "*e una bella figura*". Moreover it is very clear that the nationality of the person plays a role because it is in Italian. As a matter of fact even addressing "Capello" in Italian, "dear *Signor* Capello" is an indication that the language that we use on particular occasions can be significantly influenced by what we know about the addressee—in this case that he is Italian.

Now let me say what we can find about this, that is, the influence of what we know about the topic, the conceptualizer and the addressee in poetry. In order to give you a sense of this, again I have to recite to you a poem. This time an Emily Dickinson poem.

> I reckon—when I count it all—
> First—Poets—Then the Sun—
> Then Summer—Then the Heaven of God—
> And then—the List is done—
>
> But, looking back—the First so seems
> To Comprehend the Whole—
> The Others look a needless Show—
> So I write—Poets—All—
>
> Their Summer—lasts a Solid Year—
> They can afford a Sun
> The East—would deem extravagant—
> And if the Further Heaven—

>   Be Beautiful as they prepare
>   For Those who worship Them—
>   It is too difficult a Grace—
>   To justify the Dream—

In my interpretation, and I am pretty sure this is not the only interpretation, this poem is about poetic creativity. In particular I find two conceptual metaphors here that Emily Dickinson creates. One is what we can call POETIC CREATIVITY IS A NEW WAY OF SEEING (AS A RESULT OF THE SUMMER SUN). So we have the following mappings and this is based on the first half of the poem: the summer corresponds to the productive period of the poet, the sun corresponds to the inspiration of the poet, and the new way of seeing corresponds to being poetically creative. This already indicates that Emily Dickinson is highly concerned about a major problem that she has had all her life or most of her life which is that she has a very serious optical illness. She has to spend many of her summers inside the house. She was not allowed by her doctors to go out to the sun.

The second one is even more significant and this is what I call the POEMS ARE HEAVENS metaphor where notice that in the second half of the poem it says "and if the Further Heaven Be Beautiful as they prepare For Those who worship them." The Further Heaven here corresponds to the poem, the worshippers correspond to the people reading poetry, God corresponds to the poet, and most importantly God's grace corresponds to the poet's inspiration. This is what she says "Be Beautiful as they prepare for those who worship them. It is too difficult a grace to justify the dream." God's grace corresponds to the poet's inspiration, but her impaired vision and her major optical illness is a very difficult kind of grace. It is a grace, because she is very much aware that she can produce poetry that no one else has ever created. But at the same time it is a difficult grace for her to accept as it would be for all of us who are, seriously physically impaired in some way, but what she does is that she knows her terrible condition, this optical illness and she turns it into a beautiful metaphor to talk about her poetry.

Let me turn to the topic and the addressee. In everyday metaphorical creativity I mentioned that there are three pieces of knowledge that we can utilize to talk about, to create new metaphors: either the knowledge that a conceptualizer has about himself or herself or the topic, or the knowledge we have about the addressee. And in this particular case of the Emily Dickinson poem we saw that the knowledge that the conceptualizer, that is the poet, Emily Dickinson, has about herself can be turned into a unique metaphor in this poem.

Now I want to show that the topic and the addressee, the knowledge that we have about them can also be good to use for the creation of new metaphors. In order to show that I want to take a look at another poem by the American poet Sylvia Plath called *Medusa*.

> Off that landspit of stony mouth-plugs,
> Eyes rolled by white sticks,
> Ears cupping the sea's incoherences,
> You house your unnerving head—God-ball,

Well, I wouldn't be surprised if you did not figure out what this means. The important metaphor is "You house your unnerving head—God-ball". In this poem, called *Medusa*, Sylvia Plath is talking about her strained and very ambivalent relationship with her mother. She is using the Medusa metaphor here because we know that this is one of the Gorgons in Greek mythology, and it can kill you just by looking at you, and it has snakes for hair. So it's a very creepy sight and that is a very unpleasant person—with "person" used metaphorically. What is going on here is that the very negative aspects of the poet's relationship with her mother triggers the use of an equally negative kind of character, in this case from Greek mythology.

So we can say of course that a part of the story is that it is the global cultural context, in this case Greek mythology, that is responsible for that metaphor and that is true. However, the knowledge that Sylvia Plath has about her mother and her relationship with her mother is more fundamental in explaining why this particular metaphor is created. If she had a different kind of relationship with her mother, if her mother could be characterized by a different set of properties, if she was a different kind of mother, then she would not turn to such a negative character in Greek mythology to characterize the mother. It is in this sense that I claim that the knowledge that Sylvia Plath has about her mother and her relationship with her mother explains the choice for this particular metaphor, but of course the explanation is based both on the knowledge that she has and the particular cultural context—a part of which is that she knows Greek mythology.

What I've argued her is that there are both global and local contexts that may trigger, or facilitate at least, the use of particular metaphors in particular contexts, and of these contexts of the immediate kind I looked at the physical environment, and the knowledge that the conceptualizer has about either himself or herself, the topic or the addressee. Furthermore I pointed out that this applies not only in everyday discourse but also in the case of poetry.

LECTURE 8

A New View of Metaphorical Creativity II

Allow me summarize the argument so far that I made. In the cognitive linguistic literature, maybe the only theory of metaphor variation and especially creativity in the use of metaphor comes from a well-known book by Lakoff and Turner (1989) called *More Than Cool Reason*, where they spell out their own version of how we can creatively produce metaphors. They say that given the source and given the target, the source domain can be elaborated or extended—you can question it, you can combine all kinds of source domain. This is their basic idea.

My suggestion is that we have to go beyond these because there are many cases where creativity doesn't come from these cognitive operations that they suggest. Also, another powerful view of metaphorical creativity comes from Fauconnier and Turner who say that it is not simply the case that we map the source on the target, but the source and the target can both contribute to a third space. You know the story. And this way we can account for a large amount of creativity.

Now I would like to take this one step further and suggest that there is a neglected area here. The neglected area is that of context. The context contributes a huge amount of information that we pay attention to when we conceptualize something metaphorically. We can take advantage of various aspects of context when we conceptualize something metaphorically.

Now I will distinguish global context and local context. A global context characterizes an entire language community. So if a culture, for example, lives on the slopes of the Himalayas or the Andes in South America, that will have an impact on their use of metaphorical language compared to another nation that lives on the seaside. So this is what I mean by global context.

Immediate context, however, means the particular communicative situation in which a specific conceptualizer produces some metaphors. It is particularly

All original audio-recordings and other supplementary material, such as any hand-outs and powerpoint presentations for the lecture series, have been made available online and are referenced via unique DOI numbers on the website www.figshare.com. They may be accessed via a QR code for the print version of this book. In the e-book, both the QR code and dynamic links are available, and can be accessed by a mouse-click.

© ZOLTÁN KÖVECSES. REPRODUCED WITH KIND PERMISSION FROM THE AUTHOR BY KONINKLIJKE
BRILL NV, LEIDEN, 2020 | DOI:10.1163/9789004364905_009

this kind of context that I was talking about in the morning and I distinguish five different aspects of what I call the immediate context. The first one is the physical environment. The second is the knowledge that we have about the main entities in the discourse—that is, the conceptualizer, the topic of the discourse, and the addressee. Thirdly we have the cultural context, immediate cultural context, the social context, and the immediate linguistic context. These last three are the ones I am going to talk about this afternoon, because in the morning I talked about the immediate physical context and the knowledge that we have about the main entities of the discourse.

There is one more general thing that I should mention because it seems to be another important claim of the view that I am proposing here, which is that in the same way as this kind of metaphorical creativity can be found in everyday situations, in the same way we find this in poetic language. It is not the case that poetic metaphors are only created by the cognitive mechanisms that Lakoff and Turner suggest. It is also these immediate contexts that provide a great deal of the metaphorical materials that poets create. So I will discuss these three different types of contexts and provide examples for both everyday cases and poetic uses.

Let's begin with the immediate cultural context on metaphor use, and I want to give you an example that comes from the *San Francisco Chronicle* in 2003, and it's a somewhat long passage.

> "Arnold Schwarzenegger is not the second Jesse Ventura or the second Ronald Reagan, but the first Arnold Schwarzenegger," said Bill Whalen, a Hoover Institution scholar who worked with Schwarzenegger on his successful ballot initiative last year and supports the actor's campaign for governor.
> "He's a unique commodity—unless there happens to be a whole sea of immigrant body builders who are coming here to run for office. This is 'Rise of the Machine,' not 'Attack of the Clones.'"
> San Francisco Chronicle, A16, August 17, 2003

This passage is packed with all kinds of metaphors, we do not have time to analyze all of them. I just want to focus on the last sentence, "This is 'Rise of the Machine,' not 'Attack of the Clones,'" which is a very creative metaphorical usage with the meaning that Schwarzenegger is a unique individual and he should not be taken to be some kind of a copy or some kind of a clone. The question that we can ask is: how is it possible for speakers of English to so easily understand what the author of the article means by "this is 'Rise of the Machine'"? I am not suggesting that this is something earthshaking. What

I am proposing is completely mundane but I hope a reasonable explanation. The meaning of this particular novel metaphor comes from the fact that there are two movies in 2003 that occupied the attention of the huge number of Americans and everyone knows what these two movies are: "Rise of the Machine" and "Attack of the Clones".

As a matter of fact, "Rise of the Machine" featured Schwarzenegger. The "Attack of the Clones" did not feature him, but it is used for the purposes of contrast to show that he is not a copy or an imitator or whatever. In other words, what makes the understanding of the metaphor easily available is the immediate cultural context. Especially in California, when a new movie comes out millions go to see it, especially if it features Schwarzenegger. It makes immediate sense to them. It is in this very simple sense that I suggest that the immediate cultural context helps both Bill Whalen who uses the metaphor to create it but also the readers of the *San Francisco Chronicle* to decipher what it means.

As you can expect, this is happening on a large scale and this is very pervasive in poetry as well. Earlier, I cited a poem by Sylvia Plath called *Medusa*. *Medusa* is a poem that is about Sylvia Plath's relationship with her mother, which is well known to be strained and ambivalent. It's not a very good relationship. Sylvia Plath chooses as the title of the poem *Medusa* which is a Gorgon in Greek mythology. I just want to explain why the use of the word *Medusa* or the symbol *Medusa* is used for the mother. It comes from the cultural context. I wouldn't say that this is the immediate cultural context. This is broader cultural context in western civilization where Greek mythology plays a part and there are many people who know what a *Medusa* is and what it means to call your mother a *Medusa*.

However, this is not the example that I want to focus on. Let's read a few lines from the same poem:

> My mind winds to you
> Old barnacled umbilicus, Atlantic cable,
> Keeping itself, it seems, in a state of miraculous repair.

I want to focus on "old barnacled umbilicus". The *umbilicus* is the cord that connects the mother with the child when the child is born. It has to be cut. It is important to see that this metaphor is in immediate vicinity with one using *Atlantic cable*. The use of the word *umbilicus* here is pretty straightforward. We can explain it in a very straightforward manner. We can say that there is an extremely general conceptual metaphor for human relationships, which is "personal relationships are conceptualized as physical connections". Obviously, umbilicus is one of the major physical connections that we have with people, with our mothers and you can also conceive of it as the most important piece of embodiment that underlies the particular metaphor PERSONAL RELATIONSHIPS ARE PHYSICAL CONNECTIONS.

The more interesting case is "Atlantic cable". One thing that we know about the relationship between Sylvia Plath and her mother is that they keep calling each other. This is happening in the 60s. Sylvia Plath is living in Britain. Her mother is living in the United States, and we are in the sixties. One important thing we should know about the sixties in relation to Great Britain and the United States is that this is the decade when the Atlantic telephone cables are laid down and people start calling each other on the two sides of the Atlantic. Now I call this the physical cultural context. The telephone cable that connects the United States with Britain is a physical cultural context.

Given this kind of connection, Sylvia Plath can easily make use of this cable to talk about her relationship with the mother. Again we can suggest that the physical cultural context kind of triggers the use of the appropriate metaphor right next to umbilicus. You can say that umbilicus is bodily motivation and probably universal. However, Atlantic cable is very culture-specific and it is limited in time and space.

Now let's take another example for what I call the cultural context. Let's take another poem by another equally famous American poet Carl Sandburg. This is a poem called *Prayers of Steel*. It has two stanzas and the first stanza is this:

> LAY me on an anvil, O God.
> Beat me and hammer me into a crowbar.
> Let me pry loose old walls.
> Let me lift and loosen old foundations.

This is packed with metaphors. I want to call your attention to the metaphor "LAY me on an anvil, O God. Beat me and hammer me into a crowbar." Notice that Sandburg is evoking God here. He uses God metaphorically in this case, which is interesting because it is a reversal of the usual "concrete source, abstract target" domains. But what is going on here is that Sandburg makes use of the biblical story of man's creation. In the Bible, God makes people from clay and blowing air into their nostrils and so on, and creates man that way. Here there is another creation, another kind of creation "LAY me on an anvil, beat me and hammer me into a crowbar" and so on. The basic story is the same: God is making people and this is a big part of the western religious system, and we can say that because Sandburg shares this global religious symbolic system—it seems to motivate his use of this particular metaphor.

Let's take another interesting poem by Sandburg, which is called *Skyscraper*. "BY day the skyscraper looms in the smoke and sun and has a soul." What is important is that the poem is entitled the *Skyscraper* and we can ask what the *Skyscraper* stands for. Well, it stands for America.

Now we have an interesting case here because this is not the metaphor. This is a metonymy. The metonymy is SKYSCRAPER FOR THE UNITED STATES. More generally, however, this fits another generic metonymy, A CHARACTERISTIC PROPERTY FOR THE PLACE THAT IT CHARACTERIZES. Notice that this poem was written in 1916, which was in the decade when the first skyscrapers were built in the major American cities like Chicago and New York. Now given this aspect of the American landscape, there were more and more skyscrapers being built in the big cities, the poet Sandburg takes the skyscraper as a characteristic property of the United States and lets it stand for the entire United States. The selection of this metonymic vehicle comes from the immediate cultural context that is culture-specific and time-specific and so on.

Let's take a look at the effect of the immediate social setting on metaphor use. I want to start with an everyday example. The everyday example is interesting because it is not necessarily an unconventional metaphor, but it is an interesting and important example because it allows us to talk about the motivation of the selection of particular metaphors rather than others. I used an example earlier of a newspaper article in which an American journalist goes and does an interview with Fats Domino, a famous American rock musician who lives in New Orleans after the hurricane that devastated the city in 2005.

The interview was done in 2007 and this is a sentence from that article: "The rock 'n' roll pioneer rebuilds his life—and on the new album 'Goin' Home,' he plays his timeless music." He "rebuilds his life". Obviously, this is the LIFE IS A BUILDING metaphor. However, if we take what this means and if we ask what this means, it turns out that the same kind of meaning could easily be given by several other metaphors. Yesterday I mentioned that we have more than a dozen conceptual metaphors for life. But the ones that would sound completely natural and fitting here are LIFE IS A JOURNEY and LIFE IS A MACHINE. So maybe the journalist could have said "and restarts his life" or "he sets out on a new journey" or something like that. There are other conceptual metaphors that could have been used instead of "rebuilds his life". So the question is: Is there any motivation for this particular metaphor? I would say yes. The reason is, we find out from the article, that's why we have to look at the entire discourse to see what motivates a particular metaphorical use and why.

It turns out that the place where they are talking about is Fats Domino's house. Actually, Fats Domino has two houses, and they are rebuilding one of the houses. Maybe they can even see the actual building site where the work is done and it seems to me that it must have influenced the journalist in selecting the particular metaphor. Why do I call this the social context? Because work in general is one of the major categories of the social context, in addition to many others. So we can make a generalization here.

If you want to use a particular source domain to express meaning related to a particular target and there is something in the immediate social context that fits that meaning—and in this case it is construction work on the house—then use that source domain rather than other source domains that are not immediately motivated by anything in the context. So the JOURNEY metaphor would not be as obvious a choice. They are probably sitting in their chairs, so the MACHINE metaphor would not be applicable. There is nothing in the context that would suggest that. However, the BUILDING metaphor is highly motivated in the context and that seems to me to explain this particular choice.

Let's address the social context in poetry. In order to look at an example, let's take the second stanza of the same poem by Sandburg, *Prayers of Steel*. "Lay me on an anvil, O God." This is still the first stanza. The second one will come in a moment. "Beat me and hammer me into a steel spike."

> Drive me into the girders that hold a skyscraper together.
> Take red-hot rivets and fasten me into the central girders.
> Let me be the great nail holding a skyscraper through blue nights into white stars.

Again this is packed with metaphors. Notice that "blue nights into white stars" evokes the American flag, so there are many interesting things here. I want to concentrate on the line, "Beat me and hammer me into a steel spike. Drive me into the girders that hold a skyscraper together. Take red-hot rivets and fasten me into the central girders. Let me be the great nail holding a skyscraper through blue nights into white stars." I suggest that there is a particular conceptual metaphor here, which is THE CONSTRUCTION OF NEW SOCIAL STRUCTURE IS THE PHYSICAL MAKING OF NEW TOOLS AND BUILDING INGREDIENTS. It is the characteristically social situation of tool making and using that tool to make something else in the American context that inspires the analogy used by the poet.

When I say that the immediate physical context plays a role in the selection in the choice of particular metaphors both in everyday situations and in poetry, I do not mean to imply that what we take to be completely conventional conceptual metaphors do not play a role in the picture. They often do, although we have seen several examples where there is no trace of any conventional conceptual metaphor. If we analyze this particular metaphor further, then what we find is that, first of all, it starts with the metonymy SKYSCRAPER FOR AMERICA. Then we have another which we saw for the other poem and then THE CONSTRUCTION OF NEW SOCIAL STRUCTURE IS THE PHYSICAL MAKING OF NEW TOOLS AND BUILDING INGREDIENTS.

Both the metonymy and this specific metaphor are a special case of a completely entranced, well-established conventional metaphor, which is SOCIETIES ARE BUILDINGS. So it is not so surprising that the metonymy makes use of a particular kind of building in this case, skyscraper. It is also not so surprising that we get this very specific metonymy that Sandburg uses in this *Prayers of Steel*. After all, SOCIETIES ARE BUILDINGS is a well-known conceptual metaphor to all of us. Even more generally, what we find is an entire system of metaphors where COMPLEX SYSTEMS ARE COMPLEX PHYSICAL OBJECTS. So at a very highest level, we have COMPLEX SYSTEMS ARE COMPLEX PHYSICAL OBJECTS, like buildings. Then we have SOCIETIES ARE BUILDINGS. We have the more specific metaphor in the poem and we also have the SKYSCRAPER FOR AMERICA metonymy. They all hang together somehow and are maybe at the basis of all these is the completely conventional SOCIETIES ARE BUILDINGS metaphors.

The SOCIETIES ARE BUILDINGS metaphor is made up of the following conventional mappings. The builders correspond to the persons creating the society, the process of building to the process of creating society, the foundation of the building, the basic principles on which society is based—the building materials, the ideas used to create society, the physical structure of the building, the social organization of the ideas. The building itself corresponds to society. This is a complex image. We could call it a blend, which has several changes in the basic metaphor. The building becomes a skyscraper, the builder becomes God or the blacksmith, and the building materials and tools become the poet. Notice what he says, "Beat me and hammer me into a steel spike". So he is turned into the poet. He is turned into one of the tools that you want to use to restructure American society—to take apart the old structure and to build a new one.

Finally, let's turn to the effect of the immediate linguistic context on metaphor use. I take this example from the *London Times*. I told you that some of these examples come from the editions of the *London Times* in 2008 because I spent the winter there that year. This is one of the examples where I feel the immediate linguistic context plays a role in shaping the metaphors that we use in the text. Consider this:

When the Electoral Commission came to make its choice between referring the case to the police and taking no action, it was this defence, described by an authoritative source as showing "contempt" for the law, which helped to tilt the balance—[this is what we need, to tilt the balance] and Mr. Hain—over the edge.

Notice the metaphor "tilt the balance" and notice that we have an elliptical metaphor immediately afterward where the article says "and [*tilt*] *Mr. Hain over the edge*". Mr. Hain is a representative or a member of Parliament. He committed something and there was some debate about what to do with him—whether to report his case to the police or do something else. This is why this expression came up to "tilt the balance".

Now the expression "tilt the balance" is based on an interesting conceptual metaphor, UNCERTAIN IS BALANCE, UNCERTAINTY IS BALANCE and LACK OF UNCERTAINTY ITSELF IS LACK OF BALANCE. There is an American English expression "to sit on the fence". When you sit on the fence, first of all, it's very unpleasant, but secondly, there is the issue of which way you fall, this way or the other way. This balanced situation indicates uncertainty. However, when you fall to one side, that indicates certainty. Now in this case, however, we have a more serious situation, because the falling does not involve simply falling on this side or that side of a fence, but falling over the edge. Now falling over the edge reflects an interesting conceptual metaphor, which is LOSS OF RATIONAL/MORAL CONTROL IS LOSS OF PHYSICAL CONTROL, such as the physical fall into a deep hole. Well, this is a very ancient metaphor, just think of the biblical fall, which is, LOSS OF MORAL CONTROL and so on. So there is an interesting historical story behind it.

Let's focus on the expression again—tilt Mr. Hain over the edge. It means something like "to cause someone to fall down into a hole", when you fall over the edge and it tilts someone over the edge. Now there are many verbs, there are many verbs that could be used in the same metaphorical sense at this point of the discourse that could be used, but interestingly it is the verb *tilt* that it is used.

There are many more conventional verbs. I checked in several dictionaries and the most conventional phrase that is given by dictionaries is "push someone over the edge", or "drive someone over the edge". It's not *tilt*. In addition to *tilt*, *push*, and *drive*, you could have *force, jolt, nudge, poke, prod, propel, shove, press, butt*, and so on in the same phrase.

Interestingly enough, it is *tilt* that is used. The question is why. My answer to this is that it is used because in the same discourse, immediately preceding it, you have the verb *tilt*. The general meaning of the verb *tilt*, maybe it's not perfect, but it fits the situation. It can be used to express the meaning that needs to be expressed. Because the conceptualizer keeps the verb *tilt* in mind, as here you see it creates the discourse—if it fits the linguistic context, it influences the conceptualizer to make *tilt* the choice for the metaphor where more conventionally they perhaps could have said "drive him over the edge", or "push him over the edge". So this is what I mean by the effect of the linguistic context. The psychological mechanism behind this must be a lot more complex than I indicate.

Now I believe that in some cases we find the same kind of influence that comes from the immediate linguistic context in poetry as well. As an illustration, let's stay with the *Medusa* poem again by Sylvia Plath. Notice that the *Medusa* poem uses the element of Greek Mythology and it is based on the relationship with her mother. This is the important part: Medusa is not only a Gorgon in Greek Mythology; there is another sense of Medusa, which is "jellyfish".

We can see the "jellyfish" sense in the following quote "Did I escape, I wonder?" and "Your stooges/Plying their wild cells in my keel's shadow." All this school of jellyfish are chasing her and she is trying to get away from the mother, in this case from the "jellyfish". Now, and the "jellyfish" can harm you, so it expresses the same kind of idea that the Medusa, Geek Mythology's *Medusa* seems to indicate.

Now what makes this a case of the immediate linguistic context is that the association between the "jellyfish" sense of Medusa and the Gorgon sense of Medusa is as tight as you can get. Namely, you have sense 1 and sense 2 of the same word. We can say that the first use of Medusa, the first conventional sense of Medusa, the Greek Mythology sense evokes or activates the entire semantic structure of the word. It comes in handy for the author, in this case the poet, to continue to use the same word without shifting to another metaphor because, she wants something in which she is being chased and she is trying to get away. She finds it difficult and scary and so on. And the second sense of Medusa, "jellyfish" can provide exactly that.

So far I have been somewhat dogmatic about separating all the different kinds of context that I have talked about—the physical environment, the knowledge we have about the main entities of the discourse, the cultural context, the social context, and the immediate linguistic context. I probably conveyed to you the idea that these influences come in neatly separate ways. That is not true of what we get in reality most of the time, and this complicates the analysis further. What we find in real discourse most of the time is that many of these contextual influences show up in the same text at the same time.

I want to give you a Hungarian example. But don't worry, it's translated into English. I don't want to frustrate you with the Hungarian text. I immediately go to an almost literal translation that I provide in English. Ok, let me give you the context of this particular piece of discourse.

Two years ago, in Hungarian society, there was a major political debate about whether Hungary should adopt the American health care system or should stay with the states-sponsored health care system. What the American system means is that you have to take out insurance with all kinds of different private companies. There was a referendum about this, people voted about this. I don't know [roughly] 80% of the people voted against making use of the American system. But this article that I translated came at the time of the debate, and a doctor published a lengthy kind of essay about the issue and his views on the Internet. So I found this on the Internet and this is how it goes:

> This paper was born, or this essay was born in the period when people think about the issue. [namely the issue I mentioned] Its objective is to analyze the expected effects of the law. In its methods, it follows the way doctors think. It imagines Hungarian health care as the patient. It takes the government as the attending physician, and invites experts and the author [of the article] himself to be the consultants. It considers the correct diagnosis to be the precondition for predicting the prognosis. Finally it briefly examines if there is an alternative possibility for treatment.

Ok, I think you get the idea. This is a doctor writing about Hungarian health care and you know this is the major concern for him. So we can translate what is going on here in our terms in the following way. The author has a great deal of knowledge about the conceptualizer because it is himself and he happens to be a doctor.

Secondly, he must have a great deal of concern and interest in the issue that he is talking about. That's why he wrote the essay to begin with. Third, notice what the topic of the discourse is. The topic of the discourse is health care in Hungary itself.

These are three of the different kinds of contexts that I have mentioned so far, on which this particular author relies in producing a piece of discourse about this particular subject matter. So it seems that it is not a single kind of context [contextual factor] that plays a role and influences the choice of metaphors, but at least these three different types of context [contextual factor] that play a role in it.

Now I want to suggest that we find the same thing in poetry. In order to see that, let's take a look at the *Prayers of Steel* poem by Sandburg:

LAY me on an anvil, O God.
Beat me and hammer me into a crowbar.
Let me pry loose old walls.
Let me lift and loosen old foundations.

Lay me on an anvil, O God.
Beat me and hammer me into a steel spike.
Drive me into the girders that hold a skyscraper together.
Take red-hot rivets and fasten me into the central girders.
Let me be the great nail holding a skyscraper through blue nights into white stars.

Now there are, as I mentioned, several different contexts that simultaneously influence the author probably at the time of writing the poem. The first one is the religious belief system that I mention. This was part of the cultural context in which the poet evokes the creation of man by God in the biblical story. The second one was a particular model of work, which is a part of the [social category of] work, which is a part of what I called the social context.

Now interestingly enough what we can see is that a third kind of context also plays a role. The third kind of context is the knowledge that the speaker has about himself, namely, it turns out, if you dig deeply enough into Carl Sandburg's biography, it turns out that his father was a blacksmith, and he spent some of his early childhood in his father's workshop. We can say that there are again at least three different kinds of context that may have influenced the particular choice of metaphors in this poem by Sandburg.

I'm sure that Fauconnier and Turner would give you a very different kind of story. They would say that this is an extremely complex blend. They would go through all the different spaces and then they would come up with a blend. You know that would be fine with me. However, one of the main questions that comes up in connection with such complex mental spaces is *why those particular mental spaces*?

To many people, the mental spaces that they operate with are completely unmotivated. They just say that this is prompted by this part of the expression; it's prompted by the other part of the expression and so on and so forth. So why are those parts of expressions there in the poem? In other words, why do we have the mental spaces that we do, operating in the poem and in many other examples.

I would say that the kind of account that I am outlining here takes a step in the right direction, because we can suggest that the mental spaces are there because they are, to a large extent, motivated by the particular contexts in which a particular poet or a particular conceptualizer puts together the conceptual materials for, in using metaphors. So in other words, we can find some non-linguistic kind of motivation for why we have the particular mental spaces that we do.

So let me turn to my final large issue, which is: What are the sources of metaphorical creativity? The answer should be obvious on the basis of what I have been talking about so far, which is that in addition to the kind of creativity that is provided by Lakoff and Turner in the sense of particular operations on the source domain, that is source-related creativity. In addition to the kind of system that Fauconnier and Turner suggest, which is the network model, I think there is a third large set of sources that can produce novel metaphors and that in some cases can motivate the use of conventional metaphors in real discourse.

The immediate linguistic context is produced by a particular speaker or conceptualizer about a particular topic and to a particular addressee—another conceptualizer. All of this is embedded in at least three contexts, three different contexts, what I called the cultural context, the social context, and the physical environment. The core idea of all this is that in addition to motivation for the use of metaphors and especially creative metaphors, in addition to what cognitive linguists so far have focused on, which is what we called the pressure of coherence and, within that, the pressure of the body, there is another kind of pressure that I call the pressure of context, and the pressure of context seems to me to be a valuable tool to explain many of the non-universal uses of metaphors.

What can we say about all this by way of conclusions? First of all, I would like to say that we can distinguish at least largely two kinds of context: global context and local context. Within the local context, there is what is called immediate linguistic context, knowledge that we have about the main entities, immediate cultural context, immediate social context, immediate physical setting. This is what I call context. These produce what I call context-induced metaphors.

Now if this idea proves to be correct—and I am aware that a lot more evidence is needed—then I think we have something important to add to standard conceptual metaphor theory where two basic types [of metaphors] are distinguished. One is metaphors that are based on some kind of resemblance and metaphors based on some kind of correlation. Metaphors that are based on some kind of correlation are called primary metaphors. This is what the standard view maintains. These are the main two types of metaphor. If I am correct, and we can think of these examples the way I suggested, then there is a third kind of metaphor, and I call it context-induced metaphors.

This kind of approach has certain implications for the analysis of poetry as well. And so it has implications for cognitive poetics. One implication is that it is common in literary circles to distinguish two basic approaches to a poem. One is a hermeneutical-postmodernist kind of approach, which examines a poem as a whole and doesn't go beyond the poem. It tries to figure out what the poem means, given the role of the poem is, given the role of the poem.

Another kind of approach, which is a more traditional kind of approach, emphasizes the social, cultural, and personal background of a poem. In other words, the second approach maintains that in order to understand the poem, we need to understand, the various social, cultural, personal, and other issues in the background of the poem. I think this kind of analysis gives us a nice way of combining the two approaches in a natural way. We can look at the context in the way I have and examine its influence and see how the metaphors that derive from those contexts can shape the internal interpretation of each and every poem. I would imagine that it would be very difficult to understand either the Sandburg poem *Prayers of Steel* or the Sylvia Plath poem, without looking at the cultural and contextual factors and try to figure out the meaning without them.

Lakoff and Turner suggest that what distinguishes a poetic metaphor from an everyday metaphor is that in poetic metaphors poets take particular conventional conceptual metaphors like DEATH IS SLEEP from Hamlet, and Shakespeare takes this further when he says, "To die, to sleep, perchance to dream." That is, the author can elaborate or extend the metaphor, go beyond the SLEEP source domain.

However, others have pointed out that in everyday uses of metaphor, we find the same conceptual devices to produce novel metaphors. So then the question arises: how can we explain what is unique about poetic metaphor? And on the basis of my talk at least, I think you would agree with me that it is not only the conceptual devices like extension, elaboration, questioning, and so on that are shared by forms of everyday uses of metaphor and poetic metaphor in poetry, but also what we find is that all the contextual factors that I have talked about are common to or are shared by both everyday and poetic uses of metaphor. So if that is the case, how can we distinguish poetic metaphor from everyday metaphor?

The only suggestion I can make to this effect is that the only difference that I find between poetic metaphor and everyday metaphor is that we find metaphors much more densely in poetic language than in everyday language. If you think about the Sandburg poem, there is an unbelievable amount of metaphor in that poem—and also an unbelievable amount of complexity. So the way I see it on the basis of this kind of research, the only difference between everyday language and poetic language in terms of metaphor is that poetic language displays a lot more density of metaphors and a lot more complexity of metaphors than everyday language. Otherwise, the same contextual factors operate there as well.

It is interesting that the notion of embodiment in Cognitive Linguistics is usually discussed as something universal. Image schemas have universal bodily bases and so on and so forth. However, in the morning I talked about an interesting use of embodied metaphor. There is a poem in which Emily Dickinson creates a novel metaphor on the basis of her own optical illness. She has a major physical problem with her vision and she turns it into a beautiful metaphor to capture poetic creativity.

This is personal embodiment. It is not the case that all of us have that kind of thing. This is not something universal. This is personal embodiment. So I would conclude on the basis of this, and I would imagine that, this is characteristic, as a matter of fact I do know, that this is characteristic of many other poets like Milton, for example, who also had difficulties with vision, albeit a different type of difficulty. There is a vast literature on this. The notion of embodiment should be extended in Cognitive Linguistics to include not only universal cases of embodiment, but personal cases of embodiment, because it is these personal forms of embodiment that can often explain a particular author's or poet's very unique metaphors.

LECTURE 9

Metaphor and Metonymy in Language Teaching

Let's discuss metaphor theory and the teaching of idioms from a cognitive linguistic point of view. I chose this topic for several reasons. One is that the issue of idioms has been with us in the Cognitive Linguistic study of metaphors ever since the inception of Cognitive Linguistics in the early years. Secondly my other major motivation for wanting to talk about this is that I was myself a teacher of English in Hungary and I always had this idea that it would be nice to be able to take advantage of what I know about conceptual metaphor theory and make somehow that knowledge useful to the wider community of teachers of English in Hungary and possibly in other countries.

With that goal in mind, I began to think a little bit about this issue of how can we make the teaching of idioms, which is a huge field itself in the teaching of foreign languages, more systematic than the way things stand today. Although there are all kinds of very important new developments here, for example, even some dictionaries, like the MacMillan Dictionary of English, gives you groups of metaphors, systematizes them and so on—but I feel we have to go way beyond this, and our ultimate goal as teachers of English should be to take advantage of conceptual metaphor theory and build what we know about metaphors into the teaching of idioms for learners of English as a foreign language. So there are four large issues that I will explore here today. They all have to do with the motivation of idioms. You will see what I mean by motivation as we go along, and I will try to say something about the applicability of what we found for foreign language teaching.

The four general issues are the following. How and to what degree are idioms motivated in one language? The second one: how and to what degree are idioms motivated in relation to two languages? How do different languages express idiomatic meanings? And four: how and to what degree do the cultural ideological backgrounds underlying particular languages play a role in

All original audio-recordings and other supplementary material, such as any hand-outs and powerpoint presentations for the lecture series, have been made available online and are referenced via unique DOI numbers on the website www.figshare.com. They may be accessed via a QR code for the print version of this book. In the e-book, both the QR code and dynamic links are available, and can be accessed by a mouse-click.

the expression of idiomatic meanings? So these are the four large issues that I want to explore.

However, before I go on to the four large issues, I would like to deal with two much more specific issues, because I do not want to suggest that it is only the issue of motivation and what motivates metaphor-based idioms and, the use of this in English language teaching that is important. There are many other areas of Cognitive Linguistics and also conceptual metaphor theory. I want to draw your attention to two such specific cases before we move on to the more systematic large-scale studies.

So the first one has to do with whether what we know about image schemas in general can help us with the teaching of idioms. One way in which I think image schemas can be extremely useful in the teaching of idioms is the following. Several applied linguists borrowed an important term from cognitive psychology that is called "dual coding". Dual coding is the association of a word or expression with an image.

To see the usefulness of dual coding, take for example, the idiomatic expressions in English "figure out", "point out", and "find out". One of the leading applied linguists Frank Boers suggests that by looking at dual coding here, there are these verbal expressions—these idioms and there is an image schema underlying these idioms and it turns out that the image schema that underlies the idioms is exactly the same, and the specific image schema is that of a container with something inside it.

So notice what happens. If you have an image schema like a container with something inside it, then you look at the container and you do not see what is inside it. However, if this thing moves out of the container, then you can see it. So this is the image schematic kind of motivation of a well-known conceptual metaphor, which is KNOWING IS SEEING. So if you take into account these two things on the one hand, KNOWING IS SEEING, the image schematic basis of this container with something inside, nothing visible first, moves out, becomes visible later, then we can explain systematically the meaning or the meanings of these particular expressions, like "figure out", "point out", and "find out". The meaning would be something like "to get to know something". You could explain why the word *out* occurs in all of them. This kind of small-scale systematicity could be extremely useful. For facilitating students understanding of similar expressions. So this is just nice example of how we can make use of dual coding, and image schemas in the teaching of particular idioms in English.

Now the second example is completely unrelated to this. It has to do with poetic language. My suggestion here is that when we teach foreign languages like English in the Hungarian or Chinese context, one of the main goals is that students should be able to read and understand and appreciate poetic language. Now one of the most beautiful examples of poetic language in English is claimed to be the following two lines:

> Now cracks a noble heart. Good night, sweet prince,
> And flights of angels sing thee to thy rest!

Horatio says this line at Hamlet's deathbed in *Hamlet*. You want students to read let's say that play and you want them to really appreciate not only the meaning but also the beauty of such lines as these two. The appreciation of the beauty of these lines is unthinkable without knowing something about conceptual metaphor theory. The reason for this is that these two lines are based on a large number of different conceptual metaphors that you rely on when you understand the meaning of the sentences.

The first line "Now cracks a noble heart" is based on two interesting conceptual devices, a metaphor and a metonymy. The metaphor is LIFE IS A FLUID IN A CONTAINER. So if the container breaks, the fluid comes out, and the person dies. The other is a metonymy where the heart stands for the person. And if the heart cracks, the person dies. The other one is "Good night, sweet prince", "Good night". This is something that we use before we go to bed, so this has to do with two metaphors. One is that DEATH IS NIGHT, but also DEATH IS SLEEP. You go to sleep. "Sweet prince", *sweet* is based on the metaphor THE OBJECT OF LOVE IS SWEET, and there are many other examples for this in English, like sweetie, sweetie pie, honey, and so on. There are a lot of them. And *prince* can be a small child, and so the object of love can also be conceptualized as a small child. There are all these metaphors that are responsible for the poetic beauty of this particular line.

Now the second line is also interesting, "And flights of angels sing thee to thy rest!" Notice that this line is also based on the SLEEP metaphor, SLEEP or REST metaphor, DEATH IS SLEEP or DEATH IS REST.

However, in addition to that, we also have an interesting use of what is known as the "caused motion" construction, when it says "and flights of angels sing thee to thy rest", *sing* is obviously an intransitive verb, but it is used in this construction and it is used obviously in an innovative way. These are some of the ways that we can appreciate and understand the mechanisms behind the lines.

Obviously, the most beautiful lines in English poetry or in any poetry are extremely subjective. This is not my particular judgment. Patrick Hogan, a major expert of world literature, makes this claim that according to some studies people consider these the most beautiful lines in English poetry. That is not the issue that I am dealing with here. The issue is what it is that might possibly lead some people to make such a judgment about these two lines, and my suggestion would be that this is packed with these metaphors. It makes use of a particular grammatical construction in an innovative way and all these things contribute to the beauty of the lines.

After these two special cases, I want to turn to the four issues that I mentioned. The first one is "how and to what degree are idioms motivated in one language?" Notice that the traditional definition of idioms. Idioms are structures that consist of two or more words whose overall meaning cannot be predicted from the meaning of the constituent parts, and to some extent cognitive linguists would accept this.

However, we would also add to that to a large extent there is also motivation. It is not the case that all idioms are transparent. To a large extent we can provide and find motivation for them. It is ever since Lakoff's *Women, Fire, and Dangerous Things*, we know that idioms are motivated by at least three different types of conceptual structures—either conceptual metaphor, or metonymy, or conventional everyday knowledge. I will be focusing on metaphor only. In order to give you a large-scale example, consider the following examples that have to do with fire.

> He was *spitting fire*.
> The *fire* between them finally *went out*.
> The painting *set fire to* the composer's imagination.
> The killing *sparked off* riots in the major cities.
> He was *burning the candle at both ends*.
> The bank robber *snuffed out* Sam's life.
> The speaker *fanned the flames* of the crowd's enthusiasm.

And what we find here is that different stages of the fire event are in focus. The initial stage is in focus in "set fire to", the final stage in "snuff it out", the use of an energy source in "burn the candle at both ends", the maintenance of the intensity of fire in "fan the flames", the danger of the high intensity of fire in "spitting fire", and so on. So what we find here is obviously a group of expressions that are based on different conceptual metaphors. "He was *spitting fire*" is based on ANGER IS FIRE. "The *fire* between them finally *went out*"—LOVE IS FIRE. "The painting *set fire to* the composer's imagination"—IMAGINATION IS FIRE. "The killing *sparked off* riots"—CONFLICT IS FIRE. "He was burning the candle at both ends"—ENERGY IS FIRE. "*Snuffed out* Sam's life"—LIFE IS FIRE. "The speaker *fanned the flames* of the crowd's enthusiasm"—ENTHUSIASM IS FIRE.

It is not only the word *fire* that occurs in these expressions, in addition to *fire*, there are *spark* and *burn*, and *flames* and so on. So it seems that it is not the case that it is only a single word that participates in these idiomatic expressions in the different conceptual metaphors, but it looks like it is the entire system of fire, the entire conceptual domain of FIRE that participates and utilizes the words that make up this particular semantic field. We can see this in the list of examples for each of these conceptual metaphors. You find the first one that we saw previously in each case and then some additional examples for ANGER IS FIRE, LOVE IS FIRE, IMAGINATION IS FIRE, so there are a large number of words participating in the conceptualization of these seven different target domains from the domain of FIRE.

We can say at this level of the analysis that one form of motivation that we find here is that particular idiomatic expressions are motivated by particular conceptual metaphors. This is admittedly a trivial form, or kind of motivation. I'm using motivations in this talk only in the sense that particular linguistic expressions are motivated by certain conceptual structures, conceptual structures, like ANGER IS FIRE, LOVE IS FIRE, ENTHUSIASM IS FIRE, and so on and so forth. Now we can take this a little bit further and say that these conceptual metaphors, the structure of these conceptual metaphors helps us to explain, and in another sense, motivate why the idioms and the metaphorically used words mean what they do. This further metaphorical structuring comes from what we know as mappings.

So we can look at the mappings, for example, in the FIRE metaphor. The thing burning corresponds to the angry person. The heat of the fire corresponds to the anger. The cause of fire corresponds to the cause of anger and so on. These mappings give us pretty good motivation for why the words mean what they do.

So "he was spitting fire" is an obviously intense kind of fire activity and so probably there is a large amount of heat in connection with it. We know this from all the dragon tales in European folklore. I would be curious to know, if you have the same kinds of dragon tales in other cultures, or maybe the dragon plays a very different kind of role. But this spitting-fire image comes from European folklore with the dragons spitting fire and blazing everything, destroying everything, with an obviously very intense heat.

That corresponds to the intensity of ANGER. This is an example where a particular mapping provides some of the meaning—maybe not the most detailed kind of meaning, but some of the meaning of a particular metaphorical expression, and the same would apply to many of the other cases, like fanning the flames of fire where if you fan the flames, then you make it more intense, you produce more heat, and then the emotion or whatever state we are talking about would be seen as more intense.

What we notice is something more general, namely that if we look at the mappings that we saw for ANGER, we would find roughly the same kinds of mappings for all the other six conceptual metaphors. In other words, what we would find is that the thing burning corresponds to the person in a particular state, the fire corresponds to the state or the process, the cause of the fire to the cause of the state or process, the beginning of the fire to the beginning of the state or process, the existence of the fire to the existence of the state, the end of the fire to the end of the state, or the degree of the heat of the fire to the intensity of the state.

So what we can observe here is that we can make a generalization on the basis of all these fire-related conceptual metaphors. We have seen seven of them, and it turns out that all seven of them seem to have at least roughly or globally the same kind of structure spelled out by the same mappings. It is not the case that fire is used in one way in the ANGER IS FIRE metaphor, and in a completely different way in the LOVE IS FIRE metaphor or in the LIFE IS FIRE metaphor. It looks like we have a more general kind of conceptual metaphor, a higher-level metaphor that we can call INTENSITY IS HEAT. That seems to motivate the particular specific-level conceptual metaphors, which in turn motivate the meanings of the particular expressions that are based on them.

Now I believe that this kind of systematicity would be extremely useful in the teaching of idioms. Unfortunately I haven't seen any of the English language textbooks have this kind of approach to the teaching of idioms for any language. I find this remarkable, possibly new, way of approaching language teaching, which can make a large number of idiomatic expressions highly motivated, and if they are highly motivated, the assumption of course is that higher motivation facilitates learning in general. So for that reason this could be a very fruitful kind of project to pursue.

Ok, now the second issue is "how and to what degree are idioms motivated in relation to two languages". Well of course this is even more important than the previous one, because when we talk about the teaching of a foreign language, we talk about two languages, and so here the question is, do the metaphors in different languages coincide—do languages use at least some of the same metaphors? The other question would be if they do, do they make use of the same conceptual structures like the same mappings for those metaphors that would be shared?

I did an extremely informal kind of study of this. I looked at what I call the "abstract complex systems" metaphor. I previously talked about the abstract complex systems metaphor, which consists of the BUILDING source domain, the MACHINE source domain, the PLANT source domain, and the HUMAN BODY source domain. Now I want to focus on the BUILDING part of it.

Alice Deignan, a very good British corpus linguist, works on the use of conceptual metaphor and makes use of conceptual metaphor theory in her work. As a corpus linguist, she had a metaphor dictionary published about ten years ago and she structured her dictionary of metaphors according to source domains. I looked at her dictionary and took the BUILDING source domain and what I found on the basis of her work was that, in English, theories are conceptualized as buildings, relationships are conceptualized as buildings, companies are conceptualized as buildings, economic systems are buildings, careers are buildings, and life is also a building.

What I did was take some of the examples from her work and I posted a message to the cog-ling list, asking colleagues in various parts of the world if these metaphors exist in the languages that they use as native speakers, and I got, I received some valuable feedback from speakers of all kinds of languages.

For example, I got feedback from a speaker of Japanese, who said, "Yes, in Japanese, you also construct a theory. In Japanese, relationships are built and ruined. Economic systems may be built. One's life may have a foundation;" and so on and so forth. So it was quite amazing to find that Japanese makes use of most of the conceptual metaphors that English does. I also got feedback from Brazilian Portuguese, where the abstract complex metaphors are clearly present. All the target domains that I mentioned for Japanese are also present in Brazilian Portuguese. I got some feedback from a cognitive linguist in Tunisia who said that the same applies to Tunisian Arabic. He mentioned that there might be some subtle differences in the scope of the BUILDING source domain. The scope means that you have a source domain, and the source domain may take different target domains in one language than in another. The basic ones that we have seen here, like THEORY, RELATIONSHIP, LIFE, and so on, also exist in Tunisian Arabic. And the same applies to Hungarian, where we found exactly the same metaphors as in English, Portuguese, Japanese, and Arabic.

Now it turns out that these are completely unrelated languages in the world. The issue then becomes the more specific one. Do the idiomatic expressions themselves have the same meaning across these languages? I looked more closely at the mappings—the ways those particular idiomatic metaphor-based idiomatic expressions are used in the examples sent by these colleagues.

Let's take the ruin/destroy part of this. All the colleagues mentioned the verb *ruin* and *destroy* in connection with the BUILDING metaphor. In Japanese, for example, you can have "her idealism got ruined." In Brazilian Portuguese "their marriage is falling into ruins." In Tunisian Arabic "he followed politics, and destroyed his career by his own hands." So it seems that the verbs *destroy* and *ruin* are used in roughly the same way and have the same meaning across these very different languages. That indicates that there is an underlying mapping—a generic-level mapping that is responsible for this and we can put it as for a building to be ruined or destroyed corresponds to a theory, relationship, career, and so on, to end. So it looks like universally similar experiences, like the building process, the building itself, the destruction of the building, create universal sets of meanings conveyed by the generic-level metaphor ABSTRACT COMPLEX SYSTEMS ARE BUILDINGS.

So what seems to be remarkable to my mind about these examples is that we have a relatively small number of conceptual or cognitive devices; we have high-level, generic-level conceptual metaphors and more specific-level conceptual metaphors; we have the mappings for both the generic-level metaphor and the specific-level metaphor. So we have a small number of conceptual devices and structures that can account for a huge number of idiomatic expressions in extremely different languages across the world. That is a remarkable conclusion I think, although I'm the first person to admit that this was an extremely informal kind of study—but it is a very promising one. If it is correct and if you can do it on a larger scale and you get something similar, then I think it would have very important implications for the teaching of foreign languages. Can you imagine how much we would gain if by means of a small number of such structures, such conceptual structures and devices, we could systematically account for hundreds and thousands of metaphor-based idioms across languages of the world. This would greatly facilitate language teaching and language learning, I think.

Let's turn to the third issue: how do different languages express idiomatic meanings? Again I did a very simple experiment. I took the TIME IS MONEY metaphor, or the more general TIME IS A VALUABLE COMMODITY metaphor from Lakoff and Johnson's 1980 book. Then, with a group of Hungarian students, I asked them to translate English metaphor-based idiomatic expressions into Hungarian in the most natural way that they can think of. These were MA level students—they all spoke advanced English, and there were about twenty of them. So I would think that they understood the English idiomatic expressions and they had sufficient competence to translate them into Hungarian.

Now after they had done that, we looked at four things. We looked first at the first issue of: Are the words used for the expressions of the metaphor in the two languages the same or different? Notice that obviously the answer to this is that they are different, because we are talking about the English language and the Hungarian language. However, in some cases, this might be not that obvious. There are many international words where you can find some phonological similarity, like "sympathy" is used, or there are many international words that occur in several languages. But the default case is of course if you use two different languages, then the words that are used are obviously and automatically different.

The second issue that we looked at was if the literal meaning of the words used in the two languages the same or different? That is, there is the metaphor and idioms based on it. Is the word used in the idiom, does it have the same literal meaning in the two languages or not?

The third issue we looked at was if the figurative meaning of the words used in the languages the same or different? So we distinguish the literal meaning from the figurative, intended figurative meaning and there the question was: Is it the same or different? Obviously in most cases, if the translation is good, it should be the same, because after all that's the semantic effect that you want to achieve with the translation.

And fourthly, we asked if the words used in the two languages belong to the same or different conceptual metaphors? That is, you use a particular expression as the translation of an idiom in another language and the question is: Do you use the same conceptual metaphor in your language that is used in the other language?

What we found here was that there were three clearly distinguishable patterns. The first was, it can be exemplified by the expression "you are wasting my time". These are all Lakoff and Johnson's examples, translated into Hungarian. When you translate this, what it comes to is something like "waste the time-my" where we find, we get the following pattern: the word form, obviously the word form of the Hungarian verb is different. The literal meaning is the same, the figurative meaning is the same, and the conceptual metaphor is the same. The Hungarian verb that is used for "waste" is the same, it has the same meaning as the English verb *waste*.

Now consider the second case: "He's living on borrowed time". This turns out to be a little bit difficult for Hungarian speakers. So we got two different translations for it. The first one was "every day gift for-him", the second one "got one little time as-a-gift the life-from". Now, ok, in this case what we find is that the word forms are obviously different. The literal meaning is different, because *borrow* does not show up in the Hungarian at all. The figurative meaning is the same, at least roughly, and the conceptual metaphor is the same.

A gift is not always money, however. At this stage we have to take into account the more general version of the metaphor, which is TIME IS A VALUABLE

COMMODITY. You can say that yes, a gift is a kind of valuable commodity. So in that sense, it would be the same conceptual metaphor.

The third case that we found was TIME IS A CONTAINER. I'm giving myself away. "How do you spend your time these days?", this is another example from Lakoff and Johnson, in Hungarian "with what/how fill-you the time-yours nowadays". In other words, it looks like Hungarian does not make use of the TIME IS A VALUABLE COMMODITY metaphor to express this. Instead, they make use of the TIME IS A CONTAINER metaphor in which the actions that you do are substances that go into the TIME container and you fill the TIME container with the actions that you are engaged in. So we have the following pattern for this case: the literal meaning is different, the figurative meaning is the same, and the conceptual metaphor is different.

Now on the basis of this very small-scale study, we arrive at the following frequency of the patterns. The most common pattern that we found was "different, same, same, same", that is, different words, same literal meaning, same figurative meaning, same conceptual metaphor. The second most common pattern was different, different (in other words, different literal meaning), same figurative meaning, same conceptual metaphor. And the least productive pattern was "different, different, same, different". The figurative meaning is the same everywhere because obviously the whole purpose of the thing is to provide a faithful translation.

However, this does not mean that the figurative meaning never changes. As a matter of fact, in translations of poetry and in translations of fiction, it commonly happens that the figurative meaning also changes in the course of translation.

So my suggestion is that similar but sufficiently large-scale studies may reveal which patterns are favored or less favored in the expressions of figurative meaning in relation to other languages and other conceptual metaphors. Notice that I am not suggesting that this is a general difference in the patterns used by speakers of Hungarian and speakers of English. This is just limited to one particular conceptual metaphor which is the TIME IS MONEY conceptual metaphor. You can imagine the amount of work and the enormity of a project in which you would want to look at perhaps the one hundred most common metaphors in one language, compared in terms of patterns in another, with the equivalence of these conceptual metaphors in another language, let alone several languages. It would be a gigantic task. It would require a huge amount of government grants, I think.

Now the fourth and final issue would be this: How and to what degree do the cultural-ideological backgrounds underlying particular languages play a role in the expression of idiomatic meanings? Notice what we have found so far. What we found was that students translated particular idiomatic expressions from English into Hungarian and they came up with more or less natural, acceptable equivalents. However, our impression in working on these translations was that this is only a part of the story, there must be more happening here, because we found interesting subtleties in the details of the translation, details that I haven't discussed so far.

Another metaphor that we looked at was another one of the metaphors from Lakoff and Johnson, LOVE IS A JOURNEY. Let's look at the finer details of translation. Those finer details of the translation pointed to interesting potential differences between at least American English, or English in general, and its cultural context, and Hungarian and its cultural context on the other hand.

So consider the following examples from Lakoff and Johnson "we're stuck". In Hungarian you can't really use it like this, you can't use the expression with some kind of first person plural subject, in subject position plus a verb. You cannot do that. Or you can do that, but it is somehow false or considered to be a poor translation. Most people translated this in the following way "relationship-our stuck". Or if you take "we're, we have got off the track", again you cannot do this in Hungarian. Instead you have to say something like "relationship-our got- off- the- track" or "relationship-our ran-aground".

Notice what the essential difference seems to be not so much in linguistic terms, but in cultural terms. It looks like we have a situation in which in English you have active participants in an event and in this case indicated by *we*, "we got stuck" and "we have got off the track". There's somehow blockage along the path and they cannot move on, but they are still actively participating in the thing.

For some reason, Hungarians cannot say this. We have to use *relationship* and the relationship getting stuck, the relationship getting, running aground, or the relationship getting off the track. That seems to indicate a fair amount of passive attitude to a situation like this, to a lot of situations like the one indicated by these examples. I don't know how general this is, whether it extends beyond this particular metaphor, or whether it extends beyond these particular examples, but it was interesting to see that most of the Hungarian students conceived of it in this way and they put *relationship* in the subject position instead of some active participants like in English.

Secondly, consider the following examples "we will just have to go our separate ways". If you want to translate this like it is in English, you cannot do it. What you have to say is something like "separate ways-our/our- ways separate". Another example from Lakoff and Johnson is "we can't turn back now". Again you cannot do this in Hungarian, you have to say something like "from here already no back-way". What seems to be going on here, at least very generally speaking, is that we have more active kinds of participants in English who make some decisions based on some internal judgments. There are some, they think about it a little bit and it's as if they draw a conclusion that we'll just have to go our separate ways. There are internal decisions on the basis of which they make this conclusion.

Now in contrast to this, Hungarian speakers adopt a fatalistic kind of attitude. They cannot go on together in the journey of love based on some internal considerations. They say that external circumstances don't allow us to continue on the way as we did before, and so there is some kind of difference here between the two cultures that can be characterized by somewhat different values, such that Hungarian is a fatalistic kind of culture as opposed to American English which does not seem to display that property—or at least not to the same degree.

Let's address the final group of metaphors, "look how far we have come". Hungarians could translate this sentence but—and this is indicated by a question mark in front of the sentence—they explained that, yes, we can understand this and we can say it if we force things a little bit, but this would be something that no Hungarian would ever explicitly say. The same applies to "where are we?" Again they understood it; they translated it in exactly the same way—"where are-we now?"

However, they also make the comment that this is not natural at all for Hungarian. For Hungarians, the English sentences in this metaphor seem to suggest that the participants in the love relationship somehow are looking at the love relationship from the outside. They place themselves outside the relationship and they ask the question "well, where are we? Where are we going?", and so on and so forth. That is somehow not possible to the Hungarian mind. I don't know whether the introverted character of the attitude that Hungarians have to love in this case is a good character term to indicate the different values [introverted vs. extroverted], but I think you can all see that there is a difference here in attitude between people who can step outside the relationship and look at it from the outside versus another group that simply cannot do this. This is why Hungarians find these English sentences somewhat strange.

I sent this analysis to some native speakers of British English. The native speakers of British English told me that they cannot say it either. They do not use "where are we" and they said that's typically American. We find an interesting difference here, perhaps between European attitudes and American attitudes—some further investigation could be worthwhile. So such cultural differences seem to include opposing values, like activity/passivity, optimistic/fatalistic, and extroverted/introverted in the worldview of the two cultural-linguistic communities. Again, if you really want to teach your students in a systematic way and in a subtly enough way how these metaphor-based idioms work, I think this should be a large part of your project.

The first conclusion here is that the existence of many idioms and their meanings in particular languages derive from the presence of certain conceptual metaphors and that of systematic mappings in the mind of the speakers of these languages.

Second, the existence of the same conceptual metaphor and their metaphor-based idiomatic expressions together with their meanings derive from the near-universal conceptual metaphors and systematic mappings constituting them.

Third, the linguistic expression of the same conceptual metaphor may vary from language to language. Speakers of different languages seem to have different patterns in expressing the conceptual metaphors.

Fourth, the expression of the same conceptual metaphors may differ not only in the types of patterns speakers of different languages tend to make use of, but also in the cultural-ideological backgrounds underlying the languages.

So it seems to me that on the whole we need a great deal more systematicity in the teaching of idioms in foreign languages than what is presently available. If you do successfully conduct a more systematic study, then it could revolutionize language curriculum structure and textbook writing—it would probably also revolutionize the teaching of idioms occurs in actual classroom settings.

LECTURE 10

Theories of Metaphor: A Synthesis

Unfortunately, most of the people who have done work on metaphor are not here so we cannot talk face to face. Nevertheless, the ideas are here. You are now familiar with most of the theories of metaphor that are cognitively-orientated. I am trying to undertake a formidable task of assessing the different cognitive theories of metaphor—and it's a difficult task.

I am hoping that this assessment will help us think about some of the issues involved when we try to assess the merits of particular theories of metaphor. There are some cognitively oriented metaphor theories that I want to briefly discuss and recap.

The theory of metaphor as categorization is essentially the theory by Glucksberg. There is the standard view of conceptual metaphor theory, especially as proposed by Lakoff and Johnson. Then there is blending theory, as proposed by Fauconnier and Turner. There is the neural theory of metaphor, which is a very recent one, as proposed by George Lakoff in the *Cambridge Handbook of Metaphor*. There is my version of the standard theory of metaphor, which I, for lack of a better term, call "conceptual metaphor theory as based on the idea of main meaning focus." I will say a lot more about this. Then we will very briefly touch on relevance theory—but you will see that relevance theory is something entirely different in its main suggestions.

How can we assess the different theories if it is very difficult? You don't know where to begin, what to start with. I felt that maybe the best way to do this would be to find a particular metaphorical example that is discussed by at least most of these people who represent some of the different versions of metaphor theory. If we can find an example like that, then we can see how the different theories approach the particular example and provide explanations of it.

All original audio-recordings and other supplementary material, such as any hand-outs and powerpoint presentations for the lecture series, have been made available online and are referenced via unique DOI numbers on the website www.figshare.com. They may be accessed via a QR code for the print version of this book. In the e-book, both the QR code and dynamic links are available, and can be accessed by a mouse-click.

© ZOLTÁN KÖVECSES. REPRODUCED WITH KIND PERMISSION FROM THE AUTHOR BY KONINKLIJKE BRILL NV, LEIDEN, 2020 | DOI:10.1163/9789004364905_011

Fortunately enough, there seems to be one metaphorical example that is discussed by each of the proponents that I have mentioned, and that is a rather unfortunate metaphor—"this surgeon is a butcher", unfortunate not as a metaphor but as the meaning, as the meaning that applies to that metaphor.

I will use this particular example to assess the various approaches in order to see how they are related. I will be characterizing the theories as objectively as possible, that is, I'll try to present them here as the authors themselves would present them. I'll be assuming that the theories are all valid as they stand. However, toward the end of this discussion, I will ask the inevitable question of which one of the cognitive mechanisms that the different theories employ are needed to account for the construction of the meaning of this particular metaphorical sentence.

Now I want to begin with the Categorization View of Metaphor proposed by Glucksberg. In this theory of metaphor, an entity is assigned to a category that is exemplified by or typical of another entity also belonging to that category. So if you take this particular example "this surgeon is a butcher", what happens there is that the surgeon as an entity is assigned to a higher-level category, in this case "incompetence", that is exemplified by the concept of a butcher.

So the property that Glucksberg and others use is "bumbling, atrocious worker" as synonymous. This is why it's called the Categorization View of Metaphor, because you assign an entity to a superordinate category that is exemplified by a concept that belongs to that category—in this case, butcher.

So "the surgeon is a butcher" means what it means, because we assign surgeon to the category of "bumbling, atrocious workers" and that is typified by butchers. Glucksberg would also probably agree with this categorization. As a matter of fact, I take this categorization almost literally word for word from him.

Let's take the next theory of metaphor, the "Standard" Conceptual Metaphor Theory. By "Standard" Conceptual Metaphor Theory, I mean more or less the original Lakoff-Johnson view. I should mention that the Standard Conceptual Metaphor Theory did not really look at this metaphor. However, we could easily do an analysis of this in terms of conceptual metaphor theory in the standard version of it. If we did an analysis of it, it would look something like this. We would have to set up a source domain and a target domain. The source domain would be BUTCHERY; the target domain would be SURGERY. Then we would have to set up a set of mappings where you find that the butcher corresponds to the surgeon; the tool used, the cleaver, in butchery corresponds to the tool used in surgery that is a scalpel; the animal corresponds to the human being, the commodity to the patient, the abattoir to the operating room, the goal of severing meat corresponds to the goal of healing, the means of butchery to the means of surgery, and finally, and this is the tricky part, the sloppiness or carelessness of the butcher corresponds to the sloppiness and the carelessness of the surgeon.

There is one extremely significant difference between the last mapping and all the other mappings. The difference is that all the other mappings have corresponding entities in the two domains. The butcher corresponds to the surgeon; the cleaver corresponds to the scalpel and so on and so forth. However, in a way it would be difficult to say that the sloppiness and the carelessness of the butcher corresponds to the existing sloppiness and the carelessness of the surgeon. We would have to say in the Standard Metaphor Theory is that the sloppiness and the carelessness of the butcher is mapped onto the surgeon. The problem is that we do not consider butchers as inherently sloppy and careless and incompetent. So whereas in the previous cases the means of butchery and the means of surgery are in correspondence, they both exist in their respective domains. The sloppiness and the carelessness of the butcher should be carried over to the surgery domain, but even before we do that, the problem is that butchers are not inherently sloppy and careless. As a matter of fact, many butchers are very clever and they are very good at their jobs. This is a problem and probably why no one really tried to do an analysis of this particular example by means of the conceptual standard version of Conceptual Metaphor Theory.

Blending theory then came along—Fauconnier and Turner and several other people suggested that they know what the solution is. The solution is the following. You have the usual set-up of blending theory where you have all the mappings that we have seen in the hypothetical analysis of Standard Metaphor Theory. You have the source domain and the target domain, now called input 1 and input 2, the "butchery" input and the "surgery" input. There is a generic space where a person employs a sharp tool to a body, which is the commonality between the surgery and the butchery domains.

However, in a very clever way what blending theorists do is that they say that, ok, in the butchery domain you have the means of butchery; in the surgery domain, you have the purpose of surgery. If you project the property from the butchery domain, the means of surgery, to the blend at the bottom, and if you project the purpose of surgery from the surgery domain to the right, then you get a conflict. The conflict is that if you try to use the means of butchery for the purpose of healing a patient, then you run into trouble. The problem is that you can't operate on a patient and restore the health of the person if you use the means of butchery. So a surgeon who attempts this can only be incompetent. So this is the standard Blending Theory solution to this problem.

There is a huge amount of competition between Conceptual Metaphor Theory and Conceptual Integration Theory. If you look at the Cambridge *Handbook of Metaphor* (2008), what you find is that Fauconnier and Turner have a paper in which they argue at length that Conceptual Integration Theory is superior to Conceptual Metaphor Theory. In the same volume, you will find Lakoff's Extended Metaphor Theory, in which he argues that basically his version of metaphor theory is superior to Conceptual Integration Theory. So there is a great deal of competition between these two theories and also the other theories that I have mentioned.

So what Lakoff is doing based on his new neural theory of language and his neural theory of metaphor, he comes up with what I term as the Extended Theory of Conceptual Metaphors by Lakoff. In that view, Lakoff also analyzes this particular sentence and what he gets is the following metaphor: A PERSON WHO PERFORMS ACTIONS WITH CERTAIN CHARACTERISTICS IS A MEMBER OF A PROFESSION KNOWN FOR THOSE CHARACTERISTICS. So, in other words, if the surgeon performs actions with the carelessness and the sloppiness of a butcher, this kind of surgeon will be understood as a butcher. He will be considered as a member of the profession known for those characteristics. The characteristics of the butcher are sloppiness and carelessness, so these properties will also apply to the surgeon. This is Lakoff's most recent statement about this particular example.

Now I would like to propose a somewhat different theory of metaphor along the lines of Conceptual Metaphor Theory, which I dub the Conceptual Metaphor Theory as Based on the idea of the Main Meaning Focus. Now you can find a definition of what I mean by the Main Meaning Focus. It says each source is associated with a particular meaning focus that is mapped onto the target. This meaning focus is constituted by the central knowledge that pertains to a particular entity or event within a speech community. The target inherits the main meaning focus of the source.

Although I make reference here to Langacker, I am not at all convinced that this is the same idea that Langacker has in mind. What I have in mind in connection with the Main Meaning Focus is that if you look at the standard major example of Conceptual Metaphor Theory, like the metaphors with the BUILDING source domain, the metaphors with the FIRE source domain, metaphors with the PLANT source domain, metaphors with the MACHINE source domain, what I see in all these cases is that they all have a particular meaning profile and that meaning profile can be gathered from the series of expressions or the particular metaphorical expressions that are most commonly used in connection with each of these source domains.

So what are the meaning profiles that are captured by these particular metaphors? For example, if you take the MACHINE metaphor, things like you have to oil the wheels of society, and democracy isn't functioning in this or that country, or millions of other cases, what you find is that all of these examples have to do with the functioning of a complex abstract system, in this case society. But it can be the human mind, for example, "I feel rusty today", "my mind isn't working today". These and other examples suggest that when we use the MACHINE metaphor, we use that because we want to express a particular meaning profile, a meaning focus as I call it, which is that of appropriate functioning.

In the case of FIRE, for example, the meaning focus would be what has to do with intensity. I just went through a large number of examples to show this earlier. When we look at the different conceptual metaphors that have FIRE as their source domain, 90% of the examples indicate some kind of intensity in them.

Ok in the same way, the BUILDING metaphor is all about creating a strong structure. And so this is what I mean by the meaning profile or the main meaning focus of a particular conceptual metaphor, and I am not suggesting that there is only a single meaning profile or there is only one meaning focus associated with a particular source domain. I think in many cases, there can be several.

Now there is a problem with this view. The problem is that you have to fix in advance what the meaning focus is or what the meaning profile of a particular source domain is. What I would like to suggest now is that in addition to the original definition, we should make this more flexible and think of the meaning profile or the meaning focus in more flexible ways, by for example, saying that a particular meaning focus can emerge in particular contexts. One of the contexts in which it can emerge is when you place two concepts in contrast with each other. I would like to suggest that that is exactly the case, happening in the case of "this surgeon is a butcher".

Now one of the big issues about the interpretation of this particular metaphor in the literature is whether the particular meaning of incompetence, or, as a dictionary says "a bumbling botching kind of worker" is a pre-existing kind of meaning, is a conventional meaning of butchers or not. According to Webster's dictionary, it is one of the meanings, so it seems to be a conventionalized sense of butcher. It is the third sense. Another sense of it is one that kills ruthlessly or brutally and I think this could be considered as another meaning focus of the same metaphor. It seems that different people can construe the meaning of this sentence depending on which sense they have in mind. So some people can think of "the surgeon is a butcher" probably as someone who is such a bad surgeon that he has killed several people during his operations.

The crucial question is how this conventionalized sense emerges and now that's what I would like to turn to. I would like to suggest that there is, a conceptual metonymy present here and a particular metonymy that explains the emergence of this meaning as a CATEGORY FOR ITS PROPERTY. That is, whenever you have a conceptual category that is characterized by particular features or properties, you can have the whole category stand for the properties of that category.

So you can use, for example, butcher to stand for one of its properties, namely that the butcher is bumbling or incompetent or sloppy or careless and so on. Now this kind of metonymy can be found in a large number of other cases, not only in butcher.

For example, pig or bull can be used in exactly the same ways metaphorically. When you say that someone is a pig, what you probably mean is that the person leaves a mess and is not very tidy and so on and so forth. It seems that there are many conceptual categories like surgeon, like pig, like bull, and a large number of others that can be used metaphorically, given the particular conceptual metonymy A CATEGORY STANDING FOR A PROPERTY OF THAT CATEGORY.

A further question, however, is why do we see the movements of the butcher as careless, sloppy, and imprecise, and eventually why do we see the butcher as incompetent? I would like to suggest here that we do that because we interpret the butcher's actions in reference to the surgeon's work. So when these two categories are brought together—and it is another interesting issue why they are brought together; my simple explanation is that they are brought together because they share so much and it is very easy to set up a metaphorical relationship between the two of them—we interpret the butcher's actions in terms of the surgeon's actions. The surgeon's actions are inherently considered to be precise and refined and very careful. Notice that independently of any metaphorical usage in relation to butcher, we can use surgeon in such an expression as a surgical operation, where the idea is that something is done extremely carefully with a great deal of precision.

Now given these properties, like precision and carefulness and so on, of this surgeon, in light of the surgeon, we can see the movements, the actions of the butcher as very sloppy, very imprecise. So what is going on here is that we make use of the surgeon as a background to build up the features or the properties of the butcher.

It is when we bring the butcher and the surgeon into some kind of a contrast, in a contrastive situation like this, that we build particular properties for the butcher, which is that the butcher is careless and sloppy and eventually incompetent. Now as a further part of the suggestion, what happens is that the theorized meaning, this theorized property of the butcher can now be mapped onto the surgeon. Because the butcher is seen as careless and imprecise and sloppy and so on in light of the surgeon's work, you can map the newly emerging feature onto the surgeon, and so the "Standard" Metaphor Theory can be saved with this, given this solution. You can see this in the diagram in the handout.

So what we see is that basically this is a diagram that is a blend. As a matter of fact, we have the option of simply carrying over the newly emerging feature of sloppy and careless to the target domain of surgery as in the usual procedure of the conceptual metaphor theory or we can think of this as a blend and now I have done this as a blend. What is going on here is that you have the usual mappings between butchery and surgery.

You have a generic space, which is the basis of the comparison. Then you interpret the actions, the movement of the butcher in light of how the surgeon works, and given that comparison, given that interpretation of the butcher's work, the newly emerging feature of careless and sloppy and so on will create a new source domain. Given that new source domain, we can project the feature of careless and sloppy into the blend. You now have in the blend the surgeon with all the elements in the surgery domain, except one, which is sloppy and the careless work. So this would be my way of characterizing what happens in this particular case using what I call the Conceptual Metaphor Theory as Based on the idea of Main Meaning Focus.

Now we can ask the inevitable question. The inevitable question is how do these analyses fit together and what are the cognitive mechanisms that are actually needed to make sense of the meaning of this particular sentence? Eventually there is the question of what is the best theory given the ones that I have discussed. Well, here are some of the most important cognitive mechanisms needed to construct the meaning of this sentence. We have the SURGERY IS BUTCHERY metaphor. We have the Lakoffian metaphor, A PERSON WHO PERFORMS ACTIONS WITH CERTAIN CHARACTERISTICS IS A MEMBER OF A PROFESSION KNOWN FOR THOSE CHARACTERISTICS.

Now notice that I did not make use of this particular metaphor in my way of working out the meaning of the sentence. Given the Lakoffian metaphor, you can think in the following way. You can say that the surgeon has certain characteristics, he performs work with particular characteristics and those characteristics project him into the butchery frame and because he is now a value in the butcher role—the surgeon is a butcher—you have him as a value projected into the butchery frame as a value, and because he is now in the butchery frame in the role of the butcher, it will adopt the features of a butcher which is that the butcher is careless, sloppy, and so on.

So this is the Lakoffian solution—this is a possibility. However, this is not the way I did the analysis. The way I did the analysis was that there is the butcher who is seen in light of the surgeon, as being categorized by particular negative features like sloppiness and carelessness and so on, and this feature is projected into a blended space where it will categorize a particular surgeon. So I think basically the mechanism is the same, except that in Lakoff's case, the surgeon becomes a value in the butchery frame, whereas in my solution the sloppy careless characteristic of the surgeon becomes a part of the characterization of the surgeon in the blend.

Another thing, another conceptual mechanism that is needed, as I have shown, is the WHOLE CATEGORY FOR A CHARACTERISTIC PROPERTY OF THE CATEGORY, and this is metonymy. I used this when I said that the butcher is a conceptual category characterized by certain properties and it can stand for those properties. Also there was the generic space of surgery and butchery. This is clear. This is what they share. Then there is surgery as a conceptual background to the interpretation of butchery. Notice that the surgeon in the surgery frame is characterized inherently by such features as precise and careful, and when you bring this concept of surgeon into correspondence with butchers, the contrastive situation results in the butcher being seen as the opposite: careless and sloppy.

These are the cognitive mechanisms that are absolutely needed to get the meaning of this particular sentence. We have seen a number of interpretations and a number of theories that make use of such mechanisms. Now Sperber and Wilson in their relevance theory, however, go a completely a different way. They suggest that in relevance theory, given a relevance theoretical framework, you don't need any of these. You don't need metaphor. You don't need metonymy. You don't need anything. Consider the following quote from their paper:

> The inferential path to an adequate understanding of the sentence "this surgeon is a butcher" involves an evocation of the way butchers treat flesh and the construction on that basis of an ad hoc concept BUTCHER*, denoting people who treat flesh in the way butchers do.... For a butcher, being a BUTCHER* is a quasi-pleonastic property. For a surgeon, on the other hand, it does imply gross incompetence ..."

So Sperber and Wilson suggest that, they can easily derive the particular meaning of the sentence without any reliance on blending, metaphor, metonymy, or anything. However, I would suggest that what they call inferential mechanism is very heavily based on a particular metonymy and the metonymy can be given as A CATEGORY WITH A PROPERTY FOR ALL INDIVIDUALS WITH THAT PROPERTY. So if you have a surgeon with the properties of a butcher, then that will stand for all the individuals that will have that property. I think there is a metonymy there, and it is not the case in my mind that you can ignore the conceptual mechanisms of metaphor, metonymy, blending, and so on in your account of the sentence.

So what is the final conclusion that I can draw from this? It seems to me that no single theory explains everything about the process of meaning construction required for the sentence. In this sense, the different theories fit together and complement each other in a natural way. In a way it seems to me that all these competing views in Cognitive Linguistics should naturally happen because we need all of these processes that I have talked about.

About the Series Editor

Fuyin (Thomas) Li (1963, Ph.D. 2002) received his Ph.D. in English Linguistics and Applied Linguistics from the Chinese University of Hong Kong. He is professor of linguistics at Beihang University, where he organizes *China International Forum on Cognitive Linguistics* since 2004, http://cifcl.buaa.edu.cn/Intro.htm. As the founding editor of the journal *Cognitive Semantics*, brill.com/cose, the founding editor of *International Journal of Cognitive Linguistics*, editor of the series *Distinguished Lectures in Cognitive Linguistics*, brill.com/dlcl, (originally *Eminent Linguists' Lecture Series*), editor of *Compendium of Cognitive Linguistics Research*, and organizer of ICLC-11, he plays an active role in the international expansion of Cognitive Linguistics.

His main research interests involve the Talmyan cognitive semantics, overlapping systems model, event grammar, causality, etc. with a focus on synchronic and diachronic perspective on Chinese data, and a strong commitment to usage-based model and corpus method.

His representative publications include the following: *Metaphor, Image, and Image Schemas in Second Language Pedagogy* (2009), *Semantics: A Course Book* (1999), *An Introduction to Cognitive Linguistics* (in Chinese, 2008), *Semantics: An Introduction* (in Chinese, 2007), *Toward a Cognitive Semantics, Volume I: Concept Structuring Systems* (Chinese version, 2017), *Toward a Cognitive Semantics, Volume II: Typology and Process in Concept Structuring* (Chinese version, 2019).

His personal homepage: http://shi.buaa.edu.cn/thomasli
E-mail: thomasli@buaa.edu.cn; thomaslfy@gmail.com

Websites for Cognitive Linguistics and CIFCL Speakers

All the websites were checked for validity on 20 January 2019

Part 1   Websites for Cognitive Linguistics

1. http://www.cogling.org/
   Website for the International Cognitive Linguistics Association (ICLA)

2. http://www.cognitivelinguistics.org/en/journal
   Website for the journal edited by ICLA, *Cognitive Linguistics*

3. http://cifcl.buaa.edu.cn/
   Website for China International Forum on Cognitive Linguistics (CIFCL)

4. http://cosebrill.edmgr.com/
   Website for the journal *Cognitive Semantics* (ISSN 2352-6408/ E-ISSN 2352-6416), edited by CIFCL

5. http://www.degruyter.com/view/serial/16078?rskey=fw6Q2O&result=1&q=CLR
   Website for the Cognitive Linguistics Research (CLR)

6. http://www.degruyter.com/view/serial/20568?rskey=dddL3r&result=1&q=ACL
   Website for Application of Cognitive Linguistics (ACL)

7. http://www.benjamins.com/#catalog/books/clscc/main
   Website for book series in Cognitive Linguistics by Benjamins

8. http://www.brill.com/dlcl
   Website for Distinguished Lectures in Cognitive Linguistics (DLCL)

9. http://refworks.reference-global.com/
   Website for online resources for Cognitive Linguistics Bibliography

10. http://benjamins.com/online/met/
    Website for Bibliography of Metaphor and Metonymy

11. http://linguistics.berkeley.edu/research/cognitive/
    Website for Cognitive Program in Berkeley

12. https://framenet.icsi.berkeley.edu/fndrupal/
    Website for Framenet

13. http://www.mpi.nl/
    Website for the Max Planck Institute for Psycholinguistics

Part 2   Websites for CIFCL Speakers and Their Research

14. CIFCL Organizer
    Thomas Li, thomasli@buaa.edu.cn; thomaslfy@gmail.com
    Personal homepage: http://shi.buaa.edu.cn/thomasli
    http://shi.buaa.edu.cn/lifuyin/en/index.htm

15. CIFCL 18, 2018
    Arie Verhagen, A.Verhagen@hum.leidenuniv.nl
    http://www.arieverhagen.nl/

16. CIFCL 17, 2017
    Jeffrey M. Zacks, jzacks@wustl.edu
    Lab: dcl.wustl.edu
    Personal homepage: jeffreyzacks.com

17. CIFCL 16, 2016
    Cliff Goddard, c.goddard@griffith.edu.au
    https://www.griffith.edu.au/humanities-languages/school-humanities-languages-social-science/research/natural-semantic-metalanguage-homepage

18. CIFCL 15, 2016
    Nikolas Gisborne, n.gisborne@ed.ac.uk

19. CIFCL 14, 2014
    Phillip Wolff, pwolff@emory.edu

20. CIFCL 13, 2013 (CIFCL 3, 2006)
    Ronald W. Langacker, rlangacker@ucsd.edu
    http://idiom.ucsd.edu/~rwl/

21. CIFCL 12, 2013 (CIFCL 18, 2018)
    Stefan Th. Gries, stgries@linguistics.ucsb.edu
    http://tinyurl.com/stgries

22. CIFCL 12, 2013
    Alan Cienki, a.cienki@vu.nl
    https://research.vu.nl/en/persons/alan-cienki

23. CIFCL 11, 2012
    Sherman Wilcox, wilcox@unm.edu
    http://www.unm.edu/~wilcox

24. CIFCL 10, 2012
    Jürgen Bohnemeyer, jb77@buffalo.edu
    Personal homepage: http://www.acsu.buffalo.edu/~jb77/
    The CAL blog: https://causalityacrosslanguages.wordpress.com/
    The blog of the UB Semantic Typology Lab: https://ubstlab.wordpress.com/

25. CIFCL 09, 2011
    Laura A. Janda, laura.janda@uit.no
    http://ansatte.uit.no/laura.janda/
    https://uit.no/om/enhet/ansatte/person?p_document_id=41561&p_dimension_id=210121

26. CIFCL 09, 2011
    Ewa Dabrowska, ewa.dabrowska@northumbria.ac.uk

27. CIFCL 08, 2010
    William Croft, wcroft@unm.edu
    http://www.unm.edu/~wcroft

28. CIFCL 08, 2010
    Zoltán Kövecses, kovecses.zoltan@btk.elte.hu

29. CIFCL 08, 2010
    (Melissa Bowerman: 1942–2011)

30. CIFCL 07, 2009
    Dirk Geeraerts, dirk.geeraerts@arts.kuleuven.be
    http://wwwling.arts.kuleuven.be/qlvl/dirkg.htm

31. CIFCL 07, 2009
    Mark Turner, mark.turner@case.edu

32. CIFCL 06, 2008
    Chris Sinha, chris.sinha@ling.lu.se

33. CIFCL 05, 2008
    Gilles Fauconnier, faucon@cogsci.ucsd.edu

34. CIFCL 04, 2007
    Leonard Talmy, talmy@buffalo.edu
    https://www.acsu.buffalo.edu/~talmy/talmy.html

35. CIFCL 03, 2006 (CIFCL 13, 2013)
    Ronald W. Langacker, rlangacker@ucsd.edu
    http://idiom.ucsd.edu/~rwl/

36. CIFCL 02, 2005
    John Taylor, john.taylor65@xtra.co.nz
    https://independent.academia.edu/JohnRTaylor

37. CIFCL 01, 2004
    George Lakoff, lakoff@berkeley.edu
    http://georgelakoff.com/

Printed in the United States
By Bookmasters